Beyond Belief

David Yallop

CONSTABLE • LONDON

Constable & Robinson Ltd
3 The Lanchesters
162 Fulham Palace Road
London W6 9ER
www.constablerobinson.com

Extracts from *Beyond Belief* first published in *The Power and the Glory* by Constable, an imprint of Constable & Robinson Ltd., 2008

First published in this edition by Constable, an imprint of Constable & Robinson Ltd., 2010

A copy of the British Library Cataloguing in Publication Data is available from the British Library

ISBN 978-1-84901-636-0

Printed and bound in the EU

1 3 5 7 9 10 8 6 4 2

For the victims.
Past, present and future.

Contents

Preface

A S OF NOW, MANY PEOPLE across the world would not allow an unaccompanied child to enter a Roman Catholic Church.

Those words initially appeared near the end of the chapter entitled 'Beyond Belief' contained in my previous book, *The Power and the Glory*. It is a chapter that, above all others in the book, continues to grab the attention of readers in numerous countries. The letters and emails are, without exception, very positive and invariably contain moving and powerful accounts of personal experiences. They also repeatedly ask me to return to this subject. Those requests and subsequent events resulted in the book that you are now holding. Part 1 is a verbatim reproduction. Part 2 continues the story up to the late summer of 2010. The investigation covers many aspects of the issue: the history, the lies and the secret system of cover-up that reached the highest levels and implicated, among others, the late Pope John Paul II and his successor, Benedict XVI. The financial cost to the United States Church alone since the conspiracy began to unravel in 1983 is $6 billion, and rising. The cost in Ireland is in excess of $2 billion. It will cost the rest of the world at least another $2 billion.

The spiritual cost, however, is far greater. Sexual abuse of any kind by a priest is an act that, not just physically, but spiritually is nothing less than the rape of a victim.

In two countries at least – there may be more – the unaccompanied child is safer than he or she has been for many decades. Those countries are England and Wales. The Nolan Report on child protection in the Catholic Church in England and Wales was a major breakthrough, published in April 2001 with more than fifty recommendations to protect the potential victims. The most important proposal of the report, one that was rapidly introduced, called for 'the creation of a national child protection unit within the Church to root out child abusers by vetting clergy, its lay staff and volunteers before they take up new posts'. Lord Nolan and his committee in their summary observed a self-evident truth: 'The fact is that should every parish throughout England and Wales follow our recommendations the problem of child abuse would not, therefore, be eradicated.' Certainly this is true, but it was a very significant step towards that aspiration.

Another recommendation also swiftly implemented was the need for a annual public report. The historical cover-up and suppression of the truth of clerical abuse is a thing of the past in England and Wales. One day perhaps that will be the reality in every country, and not just for the Catholic faith.

The figures for 2007, 2008 and 2009, however, confirm that we are far from an abuse-free society. For 2007 a total of forty-six allegations were received that related to forty-four alleged abusers. These cases involved fifty-three alleged victims. Twenty-eight of these allegations related to clergy, a further four related to religious, with a further fourteen spread over a variety of categories: female religious, volunteers, employees and parishioners.

For 2008, there were a total of fifty allegations that related to fifty-one alleged abusers, thirty of these were priests, with unspecified numbers of religious, volunteers, employees and parishioners making up the remainder. Unlike in the vast majority of countries, the Catholic organisations in England and Wales quite rightly included alleged abuse cases allegedly perpetrated by people other than priests and members of the religious orders, thereby underlining the fact that sexual abusers are not drawn from just one section of society.

In 2009 there were forty-one allegations of abuse relating to forty-three alleged abusers and fifty-two victims. Eighteen of the fifty-two victims were alleged to have been abused in the current year. Twenty of these allegations concerned incidents which are said to have taken place in the 1970s and before. Of the forty-three alleged abusers, twenty-six are clergy or reglious, seven volunteers, seven parishioners and three employees.

The various safeguards now in place in England and Wales have significantly reduced the risk of clerical sexual abuse of children but, as the figures above demonstrate, there is still a significant distance to go before the ultimate goal is reached. In a great many other countries, as discussed in this book, the situation is grim.

What follows will in parts not make for easy reading. Neither did it make for easy research and writing.

David Yallop,
London.
August 2010.

Part 1: Wojtyla: Inside 'The Secret Room'

ACCORDING TO JOHN PAUL II and many of his bishops, 'modern society' is to blame for the epidemic of sexual abuse by priests, monks, brothers and nuns of victims ranging from young boys and girls to handicapped adolescents, religious and laywomen. But 'modern society' is a catch-all phrase which means everything and nothing. In fact, the problem of priestly sexual abuse goes back to the second century. When Karol Wojtyla was elected Pope in October 1978, alongside the financial corruption of the Vatican Bank was the equally rampant moral corruption of sexual abuse within the priesthood. Over the previous 1,800 years the 'secret system' had evolved that had not eliminated the problem of sexual abuse but covered it up. Its efficiency can be gauged from the fact that before the Gauthe case in 1985/86 (see below) public allegations of sexual abuse by priests were very rare. The exposure of a priest either in criminal or civil proceedings was simply unheard of.

The Roman Catholic Church looked after its own, and offending clerics could not be brought before civil courts unless special permission was obtained to do so. The system was one that clearly had the full approval of Pope John Paul II. In 1983, after twenty-four years' deliberation, the current Code of Canon Law was published and among the many changes from the previous 1917 Code, Law 119 covering the need for special permission was removed. It was a decision that many of the Catholic hierarchy have since bitterly regretted. In less than two years, the floodgates had been opened. Within a decade the cost of sexual abuse to the Roman Catholic Church at every level was devastating. In the United States alone, since 1984 the financial cost in legal fees and awards to the sexually abused is in excess of $6 billion. The cost to the image and reputation of the Catholic hierarchy is inestimable.

It is very unlikely that the Pope was unaware of the scale of the problem at his election, and of the traditional response of the secret system. Up until 1981, he had ignored every request for help from victims of clerical abuse to himself and to various Vatican congregations. The origins of the 'Secret System', like the crimes it kept hidden, go back a very long way in history. Prior to 1869 when the description 'homosexual' was first coined by Karl Maria Benkert, the term used to describe sexual acts between two or more of the same gender was 'sodomy'. Sodomy was used to describe not only sexual acts between adult males but also sexual intercourse with animals and sexual abuse of a child or youth. This latter act was also frequently described as 'pederasty'. The term 'paedophile' was first used by the physiologist Havelock Ellis in 1906. Current scientific usage defines the sexual abuser of a pre-pubescent as a paedophile and the sexual abuser of an adolescent as an ephebophile.

As early as AD 177, Bishop Athenagoras characterised adulterers and pederasts as enemies of Christianity and subjected them to excommunication, then the harshest penalty the Church could inflict. The Council of Elvira in 305 enlarged on this earlier condemnation as did the Council of Ancrya in 314.

An invaluable source of information on the subject is the body of penitential literature dating from the seventh century. The penitential books were handbooks compiled by priests and used by them in hearing the individual confessions of members of the Church. A number of them refer to sexual crimes committed by clerics against young boys and girls. The Penitential of Bede, dating from England in the eighth century, advises that clerics who commit sodomy with children be given increasingly severe penances commensurate with their rank. Laymen who committed such crimes were excommunicated and made to fast for three years; clerics not in holy orders had the fasting period extended to five years; deacons and priests seven and ten years respectively and bishops who sexually abused children were given twelve years of penance.

The Catholic Church during the first millennium clearly took a more severe position on sexual abuse by clerics than it has taken in more recent times. The first millennium writings make no special pleadings on the basis of ignorance, nor do they ignore the fact that paedophiles do not confine themselves to one single act of sexually abusing a child. They do not blame the lay public's lack of morals, or accuse the faithful of deliberately tempting the priests. However, there is evidence to suggest that paedophile priests were quietly moved to another diocese. Most significantly the supreme head of the Church took notice when his attention was drawn to widespread sexual abuse by his priests and bishops, but then failed to act upon many of the recommendations that had been made.

Probably the most important piece of evidence that has survived from the early Church is *Liber Gomorrhianus – the Book of Gomorrah* – composed by St Peter Damian around AD 1051. The work denounces the widespread extent of active sodomy then being indulged in by the clergy of the day and demands that the Pope should take decisive action. Damian was a priest at the time he wrote the book.

He was highly regarded by a succession of Popes and became a bishop and then a cardinal.

The book is written with great clarity. Damian was a would-be Church reformer of a wide range of practices. One of his particular preoccupations was the sexual immorality of the clergy and the tolerance of Church superiors who were either equally culpable or declined to act against the abusers. The sexual activities of priests with young boys particularly appalled him.

He called for the exclusion of sodomites from ordination and, if already ordained, that they should be dismissed from Holy Orders. He was contemptuous of priests who 'defile men or boys who have come to them for confessions'. He castigated 'clerics who administer the sacrament of penance through confession to those they have just sodomised'. Damian assessed the damage being done to the Church by the abusers and his final chapter was an appeal to Pope Leo IX to take immediate action. Leo praised the author and independently confirmed the truth of his findings; however, his actions have a curiously contemporary ring about them.

Damian's recommendations concerning the range of punishments were largely modified. The Pope decided to remove only those prelates who had repeatedly abused over a long period of time. Although Damian had addressed at length the damage caused by the priests upon their victims, the Pope made no mention of this and instead focused only on the sinfulness of the clerics and their need to repent. Leo's response matches that of John Paul II over the period October 1978 to April 2002. On 25 April 2002, he finally defined child abuse as a 'crime'. Previously it had merely been a 'sin'. The former can be dealt with in the secular courts; the latter is the exclusive domain of the Church.

Nearly 100 years after the publication of Damian's book,

The Decree of Gratian, published in 1140, confirmed that clerical paedophilia was still a flourishing activity. Gratian included specific references to the violation of boys and argued that clerics found guilty of pederasty should suffer the same penalties as laymen, including the death penalty. Gratian's book, widely considered the primary source of canon-law history, also recommended that if the death penalty were considered too harsh, those found guilty of sexual crimes against children should be excommunicated. At the time this was a particularly severe punishment since it meant that the individual was shunned by society for the rest of his life. But no matter how severe the punishment, the crime continued unremittingly.

In his *Divine Comedy: Inferno* – written in the early fourteenth century – Dante wandering through hell encounters a wide variety of sodomites including a group of priests and a former bishop of Florence, Andrea de Mozzi, recently descended from Earth.

Sixteenth-century canon laws urged bishops to admonish and punish priests whose lives were 'depraved and scandalous'; punishments included cutting them off from all financial support. A papal decree entitled *Horrendum* dated 30 August 1568, declared, 'Priests who abuse are deprived of all offices, benefices, degraded and turned over to secular courts for additional punishment'.

The secret system that protects the clerical sex abuser was functioning effectively as far back at least as the early part of the seventeenth century when the founder of the Piarist Order, Father Joseph Calasanz, suppressed the sexual abuse of children by his priests from becoming public knowledge. One such paedophile, Father Stefano Cherubini, the member of a well-connected Vatican family, was so successful at covering up his crimes he even succeeded in becoming head of the Order. It took fifteen years of complaints against him and other senior members of the Order before action was taken by Pope Innocent X and the Order was temporarily closed down. As historian Karen Liebreich, in *Fallen Order* shows, the seventeenth-century secret system had a very modern ring, including 'promotion for avoidance' – elevate the abuser away from his victims.

Until the 1980s, John Paul II and many of his cardinals and bishops, including Cardinal Ratzinger, chose to ignore centuries of sexual abuse by priests. There is undeniably a direct unbroken line which stretches back over centuries from the present scandals of paedophile priests to the first millennium. Wherever one looks in the present furore, there are powerful echoes of the dim past.

Recently yet another secret Vatican document concerning the crime of solicitation has surfaced. The document, *Instructions on the Manner of Proceeding in Cases of Solicitation*, deals with the crime of a priest attempting to procure sexual favours from an individual whose confession he is hearing. It was published by the Prefect of the Holy Office, Cardinal Alfredo Ottaviani, with the approval of the then Pope, John XXIII, in March 1962. The document has never been made available to the general public. The distribution list was confined to 'Patriarchs, Archbishops, Bishops and Other Diocesan Ordinaries'. Among those receiving a copy would have been the newly promoted Bishop of Cracow, Karol Wojtyla.

It deals with the secret trial arrangements of any cleric charged with the offence. The document has recently been described by lawyers as 'a blueprint for deception and concealment' while apologists have argued that as the Sacrament of Penance is protected by a shroud of absolute secrecy, the procedures for dealing with this 'ecclesiastical' crime also invoke secrecy, putting the offender above the criminal law of the land. This was precisely the position that the Vatican has taken for many centuries on all acts of clerical paedophilia perpetrated in or out of the confessional box.

The 1962 Holy Office instructions for 'addressing this unspeakable crime' go to remarkable lengths to ensure total secrecy. The victim must lodge a complaint within 'thirty days' of the crime. Failure to do so will mean the victim's automatic excommunication. As the victim was often a young child, that particular directive beggars belief. The alleged perpetrator was able to 'be transferred to another assignment unless the Ordinary of the place has forbidden it'. Both the perpetrator and the victim are ordered to observe 'perpetual silence', under pain of excommunication. Again an element of the secret system has come into play. 'The oath of keeping the secret must be given in these cases also by the accusers or those denouncing the priest and the witnesses.' Chapter Five of the document, entitled 'The Worst Crime', states 'by the name of the worst crime is understood at this point evidence of any obscene, external deed, gravely sinful act, perpetrated by a cleric or attempted with a person of his own sex or attempted by him with youths of either sex or with brute animals (bestiality)'.

The 1962 document powerfully illustrates a twentieth-century Church still struggling with the same crimes that St Peter Damian addressed over one thousand years earlier. But unlike Damian the modern approach aspired to ensure that not only the crime of solicitation but all sexual crimes committed by members of religious orders were covered up as far as possible. In addition, the document implicitly acknowledged that error, vice, depravity, immorality and vile, vicious, worthless behaviour are found only among the flock and never among the shepherds.

In 1984 the first 'clergy malpractice' lawsuit in the United States by an adult woman was instigated by a Los Angeles lawyer on behalf of Rita Milla. More than two decades of

stunning revelations of sexual abuse were ushered in by one
of the forgotten victims. Like so many victims, Rita Milla
was first abused by her priest while taking her confession.
Father Santiago Tamayo reached through the flimsy screen
within the confessional and caressed the breasts of Rita
Milla, who was sixteen and planning to become a nun. Over
the next two years he systematically set about seducing
Rita. On that first occasion he told her in the confessional
that he had a secret and as she leaned forward he opened the
screen and kissed her. By the time she was eighteen in 1979,
after being repeatedly advised by the priest that 'God wants
you to do all you can to keep his priests happy . . . it is your
duty', Rita and her confessor were having regular sexual
intercourse. Father Tamayo then began to put pressure on
the young woman to make his fellow priests at St Philomena
Church in Los Angeles happy too. First one, then a second,
then a third. Eventually Rita was making seven priests
'happy'. None of them took any precautions and in 1980
she became pregnant.

Father Tamayo persuaded her to go to the Philippines to
hide her pregnancy. Her parents remained unaware and
were told she was going abroad to 'study medicine'. The
group of priests gave her $450 to last seven months and
told her to leave the baby in Manila. Rita was critically ill
during childbirth and nearly died of eclampsia, convul-
sions occurring at the end of pregnancy as a result of
blood poisoning. Her family discovered the truth and
brought both Rita and her baby daughter back to Los
Angeles. This happened after Bishop Abaya in the Philippines had undertaken to give her financial assistance,
not merely to cover her travelling expenses but towards
the upkeep and education of the baby. When that aid
failed to materialise, Rita went to Bishop Ward in her
Californian diocese, who also was unable to help. It was
only then that Rita and her mother filed the landmark

clergy malpractice suit. They sought to establish paternity, sue the priest and the Church for civil conspiracy, for breach of fiduciary duty, fraud, deceit and 'to protect other young women from the pain and suffering caused by priests who abused their position of trust'.

The case was dismissed by the courts who cited a one-year statutory time limitation. When attorney Gloria Allred called a press conference in 1984 to draw attention to the case it transpired that all seven priests had vanished. Far from following the precise steps ordered by the Vatican in such cases, the Los Angeles archdiocese had ordered all of them to leave the country and to stay abroad until further notice. It would be 1991 before the role of the archdiocese was made public by a guilt-stricken and remorseful Father Tamayo. Letters also confirmed that the archdiocese had regularly sent money not to Rita but to her abusers hiding in the Philippines.

In August 2003 Rita's baby, now the twenty-year-old Jacqueline Milla, finally learned that her father was Valentine Tugade, one of the seven priests who had had sex with her mother. This was confirmed by a court-ordered paternity test. Tamayo, the man who had manipulated the sixteen-year-old Rita, publicly apologised to her in 1991 and admitted his role in the affair. Nonetheless, the only financial compensation that Rita has ever received was a $20,000 trust fund set up by the Los Angeles Church in 1988 for her daughter and this was done only after Rita had finally agreed to drop a slander action against a bishop. The Church lawyer insisted that the fund was not an admission of liability but 'an act of benevolence for the child'.

The initial cover-up by the Catholic Church had been orchestrated by Cardinal Timothy Manning. When he was succeeded as Archbishop of Los Angeles by Bishop Roger Mahony the cover-up and the payments to the fugitive priests from the archdiocese continued. No action was ever taken against Cardinal Manning by Cardinal Ratzinger's Congregation for the Doctrine of the Faith, the CDF, the department responsible for canonical discipline, or against any of his subordinates or against Mahony and his staff. Roger Mahony was subsequently made a cardinal by John Paul II. Father Tamayo was eventually stripped of his priesthood by Mahony, not for the repeated sexual abuse of Rita Milla, but for getting married to another woman. After it had been established by the Los Angeles court that Father Tugade was the father of the child, Cardinal Mahony declined all requests for an interview, but the same week during a visit to Rome he told a local reporter, 'I have a zero-tolerance policy towards abusive priests.'

Before the recent appearance of the stillborn policy of zero tolerance, sex abuse cases, not just in California but throughout the world, were effectively contained by using the 'secret system' which had been perfected over a very long time. When the abuse of a child became known to the parents their first instinct was not to call in the police but to go seeking help from the local bishop. Depending on the evidence, the bishop would usually follow a well-trodden path. If the bishop felt that the evidence justified the priest's removal he would be transferred to another diocese. If he was an established repeat offender he might be sent to one of a number of rehabilitation centres. In the United States these included a number run by Servants of the Paraclete. They also have a centre in Gloucestershire in the United Kingdom. There are rehabilitation centres in many countries. These offer counselling and support to alcoholic, homosexual and paedophile clergy.

The more usual practice until very recently was to move the offending priest to a new location or parish without alerting anyone of the potential risk. In cases where the parents showed a strong inclination to sue, they would be persuaded to accept an out-of-court settlement on the basis of strict non-disclosure. The insurance companies preferred it that way too. A case that went before court and jury would very likely produce a far greater sum of damages than a quiet deal with the parents pressurised by their Church. Publicity was to be avoided. Apart from the damage to the Church's image and reputation, a public hearing would alert other victims. In some cases the Church would pay medical bills for psychological counselling, but not always.

Until 1985 that was how the secret system worked (and in many countries, including Italy, Spain, Germany and Poland, still functions). The case that Rita Milla had attempted to bring went nowhere. It would take a great deal more than that to shake the system and it was not long in surfacing.

In January 1985 in Boise, Idaho, Father Mel Baltazar was sentenced to seven years' imprisonment after pleading guilty to a reduced charge of lewd behaviour with a minor. Baltazar's plea-bargaining was a shrewd move as diocesan records showed a history of continuous sexual abuse by the priest over a twenty-year period. The victims were invariably young boys. He abused a critically ill boy on a kidney dialysis machine in a hospital in California. He abused another young boy in double leg traction in a Medical Centre in Boise. Baltazar had previously been dismissed from his post as chaplain in the US Navy for homosexual behaviour. Subsequently he had been transferred from three dioceses for sexually abusive behaviour. His superiors, with full knowledge of his record, took no action when confronted by distraught parents other than to transfer him to a new diocese.

Among those unimpressed with the Catholic Church's approach to the problem was the trial judge Alan Schwartzman. When passing sentence he paused to stare unblinkingly at the priest standing before him, then observed: 'I think the Church has its own atonement to make as well. They helped create you and hopefully will help rehabilitate you.'

The pace of clerical exposure was beginning to quicken. In February 1985 a priest in Wisconsin was accused of sexually abusing a number of minors. In March a Milwaukee priest resigned his licence as a psychologist after admitting sexually abusing a patient. In April Father William O'Donnell of Bristol, Rhode Island, was indicted on twenty-two counts of sexual abuse. He was subsequently sentenced to one year's imprisonment. The same month in San Diego another priest paid to settle a pending action accusing him of sexually abusing an altar boy.

The abuse of altar boys was also a trait of Father Gilbert Gauthe, who at the time of his initial exposure in June 1983 was a parish priest in the parish of Henry, in Vermilion, Louisiana. The revelations began with a pathetic simplicity. A distressed nine-year-old boy confessed to his mother that God did not love him because he had done 'bad things'. The child slowly and painfully elaborated and talked of the secrets that he and Father Gauthe shared. First his mother then his father listened as the boy began to reveal some shocking truths. The priest had been sexually abusing him for at least two years. Gauthe had also been abusing his two elder brothers. Before the story was all told, it would be estimated that Father Gauthe had molested more than 100 boys in four parishes, some of them many hundreds of times. Learning the truth as far back as the early 1970s the Church had responded in the usual manner: they moved him to another parish. An early report on Gauthe described his problem as 'a case of misguided affection'.

Confronted with the initial allegations Gauthe made no attempt to deny them. He began to cry. He asked to be sent away for treatment and said he needed help. He made no mention of the urgent help that his many victims also needed. Told he was being immediately suspended from all duties for an indefinite period of time, he raised no objection and meekly signed his acknowledgement of the written declaration of suspension. His superior ordered Gauthe to get out of the village of Henry. Gauthe's initial remorse was short-lived. When he returned to the village ten days later to collect his personal belongings he found time to contact his eldest current victim, a fifteen-year-old boy. Before leaving the parish he had sex with him.

The secret system was very much in evidence in the Vermilion Parish from June 1983 right through to the summer of 1984. Gauthe's bemused congregation were told initially that his abrupt departure was due to 'health reasons'. Moral pressure was brought by the diocese to bear on the Catholic lawyer, Paul Herbert, retained by a number of victims' families. Monsignor Richard Mouton had urged the lawyer to be 'a good ol' Catholic boy'. Bishop Frey tightened the screw, counselling 'caution' upon a number of parents, advising that they steer clear of civil proceedings to 'avoid scandal and harm to the Church, but primarily to avoid further injury or trauma to the young victims, their families and other innocent parties'.

The families of nine of the victims were prevailed upon to drop their civil legal action that would inevitably trigger wide publicity when it moved to a public hearing. They were told that Father Gauthe would be sent to the House of Affirmation, a rehabilitation centre for the clergy in Massachusetts. The majority of the families bowed to the intense pressure from their spiritual leaders and eventually agreed that a secret settlement was in the best interests of everyone. By June 1984 after six months' haggling the two sides had agreed on a $4.2 million settlement to be spread between six families with nine victims. Out of that sum the lawyers took about $1.3 million, the various medical experts another portion.

Although many details of Gauthe's sexual abuse were known, nothing had been published at the time of the settlement in June 1984. It might well have remained a secret scandal except for one brave family and their courageous son. The only way that some of the families discovered that one or more of their children had been violated by Gauthe was when a neighbour whose own child admitted that he had been abused went on to name other victims. Within the close-knit community, a list of names began to escalate. It was in this manner that Glenn and Faye Gastal discovered that their nine-year-old son had been abused.

The Catholic Church in Louisiana, from Archbishop Phillip Hannan down, strained every sinew to ensure that the Gauthe scandal remained a private matter. They sought to stop the issue coming to trial, for as long as none of the victims testified before a Grand Jury, no indictment could be handed down. The strategy of out-of-court settlements appeared to be working but neither the local Church, the papal nuncio's office in Washington nor the Vatican had bargained for the Gastal family. The parents deeply resented the secret suppression of the truth, as in their mind this treated them as criminals. They would neither be silenced nor cut a deal and were determined that their son would testify before a Grand Jury. Encouraged by the collective bravery of the Gastals, other families rallied to their cause. In August 1984 Glenn and Faye Gastal gave their first hesitant television interview. They were unlikely heroes but the impact and the effects of their stand are still reverberating not only around the United States of America but also much of the rest of the world.

The Secretariat of State within the Vatican were deeply shocked by the Gastals' defiance and began to exert more pressure, both on Archbishop Pio Laghi, the Vatican nuncio to the USA and on Archbishop Hannan down in New Orleans. Reports were coming in from many dioceses throughout the United States of other actions being filed. Encouraged by the Gastals, other victims were emerging from the twilight existence imposed on them by their own clergy. At no time did Pope John Paul II, Cardinal Ratzinger, Cardinal Casaroli or any of the other senior Vatican luminaries consider the alternative course of action: candid confession, humble contrition and public commitment to attack this particular cancer and eradicate it.

In October 1984 a Grand Jury viewed videotapes containing the testimony of eleven boys ranging in age from nine to seventeen and returned a thirty-four-count indictment against Father Gilbert Gauthe. Eleven counts were for aggravated crimes against nature, another eleven for committing sexually immoral acts, another eleven for taking pornographic photographs of juveniles and a single count of aggravated rape – sodomising a child under twelve years of age. The final count carried a mandatory life sentence. The trial was set for 11 October and as that date approached the Vatican increased pressure on Father Gauthe's defence counsel, Ray Mouton, to find a compromise that would enable a plea-bargaining deal. When Mouton, whose first interest was his client, insisted on negotiating with the District Attorney and the prosecuting counsel in his own manner rather than the Vatican way, the New Orleans archdiocese attempted to fire him. Nonetheless, Ray Mouton outflanked him and carried on negotiating.

Hannan then changed tack, after concluding that working with the defence counsel the Church had hired might be more productive than working against him and a deal was finally cut. Gauthe would plead guilty on all counts and would be sentenced to twenty years' imprisonment without parole. It was sold to the judge, who sought reassurance before the hearing that the victims who were nerving

themselves to testify and their families would be content
with the proposed sentence. The prosecuting counsel
assured the families that come what may and wherever
he served sentence, Gauthe would be locked up for twenty
years.

Despite everything, most of those listening to the proposition were still devout Roman Catholics. When prosecuting counsel murmured about the need to protect the Church
it was a done deal. On Tuesday 14 October, accompanied
by Ray Mouton, Father Gauthe entered the Louisiana
courtroom and faced Judge Brunson. He pleaded guilty
to all thirty-four counts and was duly sentenced to the
agreed twenty years. With the sentences went these words
from the judge:

> 'Your crimes against your child victims have laid a
> terrible burden on those children, their families and
> society, indeed, your God and your Church as well. It
> may be that God in his infinite mercy may find for-
> giveness for your crimes, but the imperative of justice,
> and the inescapable need of society to protect its most
> defenceless and vulnerable members, the children,
> cannot.'

The victims had been spared the searing ordeal of giving
evidence in a public arena. The Church had been spared the
long-term damage from such public testimony and, through
the dubious arrangement of a plea bargain, justice of a sort
had been achieved.

Between the end of the court hearing and sentencing of
Gauthe and the civil case that the Gastal family had
brought, great pressure was again exerted by the Catholic
Church on Glenn and Faye Gastal to settle the case out of
court and consequently out of the public's gaze. The Gastals
believed that the harm that had been done to their family

and, in particular, to their young son merited a larger settlement than that accepted by the other families but more than that, they wanted the facts of what Gauthe had done to their son laid out before the court and the wider world. Many ostracised them as a result and treated them like criminals, and there was talk that the lawsuit was a costly unnecessary expense. The Church had offered to settle out of court; it was just those damn stubborn Gastals that were preventing the whole wretched affair from being forgotten. And that for the Gastal family was precisely the point of putting their son through this emotional trial of obliging him to publicly recount every sordid detail.

During the hearing, attended by a variety of Catholic clerics including Bishop Frey and Monsignor Mouton, Faye Gastal was asked by her lawyer, 'When you look at Bishop Frey here, what goes through your mind?' Faye Gastal was a devout Catholic who had earlier testified that 'getting absolution is the only way to get to heaven'. Now she stared for a moment across the courtroom. 'When I look at Monsignor Mouton and Bishop Frey, I think of Gauthe sticking his penis in my child's mouth, ejaculating in his mouth, putting his penis in his rectum. That's what I think about.'

The worst nightmares of the Catholic Church hierarchy were unfolding in front of them. The Church was doing all it could to suppress the truth, including phoning organisations and companies that advertised regularly in the *Times* of Acadiana, a local paper that had withstood Church pressure to censor its coverage of the Gauthe affair. The advertisers were urged to boycott the paper.

'We were a close, loving family, still are,' said Glenn Gastal, 'except when it comes to the relationship which I can't have with my son as a young child. He is unable to tolerate physical displays of affection . . .' In the witness box the father broke down, then struggling to gain control he continued, 'He kissed me only if I demanded it before he went to bed.'

The judge cleared the courtroom before the son testified but the presence of the press, including Jason Berry, the source of the quoted court testimony, would ensure that the words of the child would be a matter of public record.

In the State of Louisiana a jury is not allowed to award punitive damages. The award must be 'fair and reasonable' for the damages sustained. This jury did not stay out for a long time, just one hour forty-five minutes and awarded $1 million for the Gastals' son and $250,000 for the parents. The Gastals' greatest victory lay not in the wholly inadequate monetary awards but in breaching an enormous dam. When the verdict had been announced, the lawyer acting for the Catholic Church declared that his client would appeal the settlement. They had no intention of doing so – it would have undoubtedly resulted in yet more adverse publicity – but the Gastals were vulnerable to such apparent obduracy and, as a result, the Church were able to haggle the settlement figure down. Of the eventual figure of $1,000,020 the Gastals' lawyer took one third plus his expenses.

The plea-bargaining deal cut behind closed doors called for Gauthe to serve the full twenty years. In 1998 a sympathetic judge looked favourably upon Father Gauthe's parole application and released him after less than twelve years. A few months later he was arrested for sexually molesting an underage boy and placed on probation.

Ten months before the criminal trial of Father Gauthe and more than a year before the civil proceedings brought by the Gastal family, three men from diverse walks of life were brought together by the Gauthe case and its implications. One was Ray Mouton, the lawyer hired by the archdiocese of Louisiana to defend Father Gilbert Gauthe. If one wanted a lawyer with a street-fighting mentality who would go the extra mile for his client, a man of courage as well as integrity, then Ray Mouton was the man. At times hard-drinking, at times filling the air with colourful expletives, he cared deeply about the concept of justice. To take the Gauthe case needed no little courage, particularly when some of the facts became public knowledge. Mouton believed that everyone was entitled to the best possible defence. Ray Mouton's occasional profanities masked the soul of a God-fearing Roman Catholic.

The second was Father Michael Peterson, a psychiatrist in charge of a rehabilitation programme for priests at St Luke Institute in Suitland, Maryland. Peterson, the founder of the Institute, had a boundless compassion for others, all the more remarkable because for many years he was confronted with case histories of patients without virtue or humanity. As a man with an acknowledged expertise in sexual pathologies he was repeatedly called upon by dioceses throughout the country to deal with priests who had transgressed.

Ray Mouton was in Washington to meet Peterson and explore the possibilities of his client going to the St Luke Institute for evaluation and treatment. He had been put in contact with Peterson by the third member of this triumvirate, Father Thomas Doyle, secretary-canonist of the Apostolic Delegation in Washington DC. As canonist at the Vatican embassy, Doyle had been given the task by papal nuncio Archbishop Laghi of monitoring the correspondence on the Gauthe case and keeping a close watching brief on every development. Father Thomas Doyle was clearly destined for great things. Promotion to bishop was considered as a certainty by many who knew him, a cardinal's hat a strong possibility. An expert in canon law, with other doctorates in Political Science, Philosophy and

Theology, also a prolific writer, Doyle could boast a daunt-
ing list of achievements.

The two priests were friends and collaborators but Ray
Mouton was unknown to them until the Gauthe case. As
Father Peterson discussed the various treatment options
that were available at St Luke's, the lawyer talked not
only of his own client but other priests in Louisiana who
were paedophiles, men whose crimes had been covered
up by the diocese, men who still held positions of trust
among their unknowing communities. As always with
Mouton, his primary concern was not to alert Catholic
officialdom but to protect his client. If it became public
knowledge that the Gauthe case was not unique, the
District Attorney Nathan Stansbury would be unlikely
to take a soft approach on Gauthe in any plea-bargaining
scenario. Any chance of Father Gauthe being merely
hospitalised or confined in a secure facility where he
could receive treatment would fly out of the window.
Because of his professional work, Father Peterson was
already aware that there were other paedophiles within
the ranks of the clergy and not just in Louisiana. He
phoned Father Doyle, telling him that the three of them
urgently needed to hold a meeting.

As Doyle listened to the two men detailing other paedo-
philic activity in Lafayette and much further afield, he was
shocked. As the eyes and ears of the Vatican on the Gauthe
case, he had assumed that this was an isolated case. As
Peterson talked of the information he had received from
'confidential sources' of priests 'all over the USA who have
sexually abused children' the three men rapidly realised that
a bishop with a legal background should be sent to manage
the Gauthe crisis and that urgent action was needed to
address the problem at a national level.

After briefing Archbishop Laghi and senior officials within the Vatican it was agreed to send Bishop Quinn of

Cleveland to Lafayette. With the Gauthe civil case looming, it was apparent to all three men that the Catholic Church in the United States was about to confront an unimaginable disaster and that the sooner they were aware of that fact and prepared to meet it, the better. Tom Doyle recalled,

> 'Within a short time we had decided to collect information and put together a manual or a book that would be set up in a question and answer format. The full edition would also contain copies of several medical articles about paedophilia. Most of these were taken from medical journals and several were authored by Dr Fred Berlin of the Johns Hopkins University Hospital Sexual Disorders Clinic.'

The 100-page document was a detailed guide to damage limitation for the American Church hierarchy. It was also an attempt to make those who controlled the Church face reality. The authors believed that the days of the cover-up, of reliance on Catholic judges and attorneys and favourably disposed newspaper, television and radio proprietors were numbered. The manual dealt with every conceivable aspect of the problems confronting a bishop when allegations of sexual child abuse were made against one of his priests or a member of one of the religious orders. Without specifically identifying the Gauthe case, the writers drew on the fiscal implications of that 'catastrophe' the cost of which 'exceeds $5 million and the projected cost of the civil cases in that diocese alone is in excess of $10 million'.

The authors, three men whose motivation in creating this document was to protect the Catholic Church, did not pull their punches:

'It is not hyperbolic to state that the dramatic description of the actual case [the Gauthe case] referred to above is indicative that a real, present danger exists. That other cases exist and are arising with increased frequency is evidenced by reports of same. If one could accurately predict, with actuarial soundness, that our exposure to similar claims, namely one offender and fifteen or so claimants, over the next ten years could be restricted and limited to the occurrence of one hundred such cases against the Church then an estimate of the total projected losses for the decade could be established of one billion dollars.'

The authors subsequently described that figure as 'a conservative cost projection'. History was to prove them correct. One section entitled 'Clergy Malpractice' predicted that as lawyers began to exhaust medical malpractice as a source of income they would see the Roman Catholic Church in the USA as a 'potential deep pocket'. Over the ensuing years, many a lawyer in the United States has grown rich from the litigation they have undertaken on behalf of the sexually abused. A number of victims living in Boston have alleged to me that their respective lawyers not only took a substantial part of the settlement figure as their fee, plus more for their expenses, but that they also received from the archdiocese a 'commission' for persuading their client to settle at a specified amount. As one victim put it: 'As a boy I was screwed by my priest. As a man I was screwed by my lawyer.' Independent evidence that substantiates these allegations has proved elusive.

The authors predicted a monstrous explosion of problems for the Church: hundreds of people going public with accusations of appalling crimes, bishops ineptly handling the response and a bill of over $1 billion. In making such a warning the two priests had done no favours to their careers. They had therefore attempted to take out some insurance of their own. As previously recorded, Doyle and Peterson had the Pope's personal representative, Archbishop Laghi, on side and Bishop Quinn was already attempting a damage-limitation exercise in Louisiana. Quinn had been selected by senior members of the Vatican. It would be some time before Father Doyle learned that Quinn's brief was exclusively directed towards ensuring that the Catholic Church should evade its moral and legal responsibilities. At a subsequent convention in Ohio, Quinn recommended that every diocese in the United States should send their files on 'problem' priests to the Vatican Embassy in Washington, thereby putting the evidence beyond legal reach. In May 1985, shortly before the report was completed, Father Peterson had a private meeting with Cardinal Krol of Philadelphia, the most powerful man in the US Catholic Church. More than any other Prince of the Church, Krol was responsible for the election of Karol Wojtyla to the papacy. The two men were in constant and intimate contact, and through Krol, the Pope was kept fully briefed on the unfolding scandal. Krol was impressed with the Manual and praised it fulsomely. He saw it as an invaluable contribution – as indeed did a number of bishops, and Cardinal Krol personally handed the Pope a copy of the report in the spring of 1985. Another who saw great value in the work was Cardinal Law of Boston.

The Vatican response both to the Manual and its implications was to apply the Polish solution. Pope John Paul II always believed that the Church should deal with its problems in 'a special room' behind closed doors. Now he urged Krol and his fellow American cardinals and bishops to deal with this 'essentially American problem' discreetly; the secret system would be maintained.

The Manual had little to do with justice: for the victims

and their families that was dealt with in less than half a page. Though concise it was, however, highly pertinent. It talked of the 'sexual abuse of children by adults' having

> 'long-lasting effects that go well into adulthood, not only physiological effects but also the spiritual effects since the perpetrators of the abuse are priests and clerics. This will no doubt have a profound effect on the faith life of the victims, their families and others in the community.'

The authors also talked of the need for direct approaches to be made to the families in question saying, 'There should be some form of healing if possible between the priest and the family . . .'

Cardinal Law told the authors that he would get the Manual taken up by the National Conference of Catholic Bishops – NCCB – by creating a special ad hoc committee of his own. Archbishop Levada, Secretary to the Committee, soon indicated that they were making progress yet rapidly Church politics and bitchiness intervened. Levada told Father Doyle that the project was being shut down because another committee 'was going to deal with the issue and a duplication of effort would not make the other committee look good'. In fact a member of the NCCB executive had taken an intense dislike to Father Doyle and this lay behind the deliberate killing of the one chance for the US Church to conduct a decent salvage operation.

Announcements, a mere PR exercise, were made at a press conference that a committee had been established to study the issue of sexual abuse by clerics. There was no such committee and at no time did anyone within the NCCB make contact with any of the authors. Meanwhile meltdown was already occurring. Four years later, with the country awash with the scandal of child-abusing priests, the executive member was still grossly misrepresenting both the document and its authors' intentions.

The collective response of the bishops of the United States was of men in denial and yet the authors of the Manual had been told by several bishops that clerical child-abuse was an inevitable topic of conversation whenever bishops met. Most bishops remained so in thrall with the secret system that they could imagine no alternative.

Pope John Paul's observation that clerical sexual abuse was 'exclusively an American problem' was rapidly contradicted by exposures in country after country. In 1988 in Newfoundland, Canada, a scandal which began with allegations of sexual abuse by two parish priests grew until 10 per cent of the clergy were implicated. The following year the Mount Cashel boys' home in St John's, Newfoundland, was the focus of a sexual abuse scandal that implicated the Christian Brothers Congregation, the Church hierarchy and the province in a cover-up that had continued for many years. The abuses of the children had been perpetuated systematically since before the Second World War. Subsequently the Christian Brothers would be exposed as a brutal congregation, many of whose members were simultaneously sexually abusing and savagely punishing the children in their 'care' in Ireland, Canada and Australia.

Just as in Louisiana, in Canada one case led to another then another. There were criminal trials, civil actions, and an internal investigation by the Catholic Church and ultimately a Royal Commission by the Government. The official transcripts of the Royal Commission and the Law Commission of Canada make for some of the grimmest reading imaginable. It transpired that Mount Cashel was not an isolated example of the physical and sexual abuse of the most vulnerable section of Canada's society. Over thirty institutions stood condemned. In its introduction, the report observed that the institutions examined in the inventory are the 'tip of the iceberg'. It continued: 'The problem is pervasive; abuse is prevalent in all different types of facilities and it extends to government-operated and/or funded institutions throughout the country.' What follows is a selection of verbatim extracts from that 'tip of the iceberg'.

'*Mount Cashel Orphanage.*

Perpetrators of the Abuse: The Christian Brothers. Both priests and the Superintendent of the orphanage committed abusive acts on many students. In the Royal Commission Report, Justice Hughes stated that the offensive acts, caused by "cruelty" and "lust" tended "to corrupt their childhood and destroy its happiness". Some of the acts committed by the Christian Brothers included forced mutual fellatio, buggery, forced mutual masturbation, fondling of the students' genitalia, "inappropriate" kissing, and insertion of fingers in rectum. The sexual abuse often began with kindness and demonstration of affection.

Excessive corporal punishment was suffered by many students, some as young as five years old, at the orphanage. The acts were often sadistic and the discipline was frequently arbitrary. For example, Brother Burke "mercilessly" beat a nine-year-old child on his back and his buttocks for losing a library card. Strapping was often violent and insensate with bruising and blistering of hands and arms up to the elbow joint, and frequently laid on, not systematically but with furious anger. Beating was in the main hitting the bare buttocks with a strap or stick but went as far as punching, kicking and banging heads against the wall.'

There had been previous attempts to investigate Mount Cashel. In 1975, the Federal Government was finally obliged to act via its Department of Health and Welfare to investigate the institute. Evidence was laid before the Department that a regime of sustained physical brutality and sexual abuse operated at Mount Cashel, but the liaison official Robert Bradley ignored the allegations. Later the same year he received another report repeating the allegations. Bradley reported to his government superior that he was perplexed as he had been *'instructed not to interfere with the affairs of Mount Cashel'*. [Author's italics.]

Before the end of 1975 police detectives visited the school and apart from interviewing boys who were extremely fearful managed to establish a prima facie case that the range of offences described above had been perpetrated. The two detectives sought permission from their police superiors to arrest the two Brothers, who later confessed their crimes, and charge them. The then Chief of Police of the Royal Newfoundland Constabulary, John Lawlor, ordered the senior police officer Detective Hillier to *excise all references to sexual abuse* from his reports, despite the fact that the investigation was incomplete and that more than twenty-five boys had made complaints to the police of physical and sexual abuse. The police were ordered to stop the investigation. The abuse was allowed to continue without hindrance for more than a further thirteen years.

There are similar details covering the other twenty-nine institutions. The number of victims runs into many hundreds and these are merely the ones that the Federal Government was able to identify. It is officially accepted that a great many more victims of these institutions will never be known. Paedophile 'clans' of Catholic priests in Canada are not confined to state-run institutions. A clan involving at least twelve men, three of them priests, a further two Roman Catholic lawyers, another who was a Brother teaching at a Catholic school and a Catholic physician was only uncovered in 1996 after functioning for the best part of a decade in the Diocese of Alexandria

Cornwell in Ontario. Its final exposure owed much to one incorruptible police officer, Constable Perry Dunlop. With great courage he established a corrupt conspiracy between his own police force and the paedophiles. Eventually twelve men were finally charged with offences involving indecent assault and gross indecency.

In 1988 time was finally called on Mount Cashel but Louisiana was offering yet a further example of the cancer within the Catholic priesthood. When, by accident, a huge collection of commercially produced child pornography was discovered in his room at a Parish Church in New Orleans, Father Dino Cinel was already on his way to Italy for a Christmas holiday. Also found were some 160 hours of homemade videotapes. If possession of the first stack was a criminal offence with a mandated prison sentence, the second hoard should have ensured Cinel's removal from society for many years.

The videocassettes showed Father Cinel engaged in a number of sexual acts with a variety of male partners including at least seven underage boys. After the Gauthe affair one would have expected the local hierarchy to act with alacrity. It took three months for the archdiocese to turn the material over to the District Attorney's office. During that time the Archbishop and his staff suppressed the fact that there was an active paedophile in one of the parishes. District Attorney Harry Connick Senior sat on the file for more than two years. He later admitted during a television interview that he had not filed charges against Cinel because he did not want 'to embarrass Holy Mother the Church'.

Despite orchestrated cover-ups by the Catholic Church, the deliberate suppression by elements of the media who were vulnerable to pressure from the Church hierarchy, devout District Attorneys, judges and police officers seeking to protect 'the good name of the Church', the truth was getting out and not only in North America. The abuse was not confined to one continent. To even confront a fragment of the evidence that I have acquired over the past five years is to journey to the heart of darkness. Priests and, in some instances, bishops and cardinals have been disgraced in country after country. Egardo Storni, the Archbishop of Santa Fe in Argentina, resigned after being accused of abusing at least forty-seven seminarians. He said his resignation did not signify guilt. Bishop Franziskus Eisenbach of Mainz, Germany, resigned after being accused of sexually assaulting a female university professor during an exorcism. Yet he denied the allegation. In Ireland, Bishop Brendan Comiskey resigned after his use of 'the secret system' came to light. In Poland a close friend of the Pope's, Archbishop Juliusz Paetz of Poznan, resigned after allegations that he had made sexual advances to young clerics became public knowledge. Paetz denied the allegations, declaring he was resigning 'for the good of the Church'. In Wales, Archbishop John Aloysius Ward was forced by the Pope to resign after continuing public criticism that he had ignored warnings about two priests later convicted of child abuse.

In Scotland, among a plethora of cases that shocked the most hardened, a brilliant crusade by Marion Scott of the *Sunday Mail* and a three-year police enquiry exposed abuse at one of the schools run by the De La Salle Brothers. Subsequent evidence made it clear that abuse at St Ninian's school at Gartmore in Stirlingshire was typical of schools run by the Order in many countries. What occurred at St Ninian's took place between the late 1950s and 1982. In Australia, the De La Salle Brothers were involved in similar activities as far back as 1911.

In St Ninian's the monks varied the regular beatings, rapes and the gamut of sexual abuses of the boys with their own version of torture and brutality. An electric generator was set up in the boot room where boys were forced to hold onto the bare wires leading from the machine and receive a series of electric shocks. The children were also subjected to whippings with a riding crop, the ends tied to cause greater pain. Christopher Fearns, a social worker, recalled,

> 'I was beaten with the riding crop two or three times a week for four years. They told us they'd whip the Devil out of us. I was battered so many times on my head and ears I cannot hear a thing on my left side, and I've undergone extensive surgery because of it.'

To date just three people have been brought to trial; all were found guilty. Among the ten charges that were proved against Brother Benedict were assault, forcing children to eat their own vomit and breaking a boy's arm. The three men were given token sentences of two years' imprisonment. Brother Benedict appealed and was granted bail. More than a year later his appeal has yet to be heard and he walks freely among his fellow citizens.

Jimmy Boyle, formerly the most feared man in Scotland, recalled his years in another De La Salle school, St John's in Springboig:

> 'Even today I can still hear the sounds of breaking bones as a monk deliberately smashed a child's leg to smithereens. Or footsteps in the night that heralded yet another horrific rape of a terrified, crying child.'

In 1999 the Sisters of Mercy faced over 100 charges of abuse in the High Court of Dublin. At exactly the same time in England, Father David Crowley was being sentenced to nine years' imprisonment after pleading guilty to fifteen charges of sexual abuse on a child under ten years old and a number of boys under sixteen years of age.

Many of his victims were altar boys. His offences occurred at parishes in West Yorkshire, Northern England and Devon between July 1981 and August 1992. On at least two separate occasions complaints were made by the parents of victims. Crowley was sent for counselling. He was then allowed to continue working on condition he *restricted his access to young people.* [Author's italics.] On one occasion Crowley watched as he encouraged a nine-year-old boy to perform an indecent act upon a thirteen-year-old boy.

Prosecuting Counsel Peter Benson told the court,

'The abuse was systematically contrived and the Crown say the accused cleverly exploited his position of trust and authority as a Catholic priest to seduce impressionable young boys. He would set about winning their trust by allowing them to smoke and plying them with alcohol as a prelude to seducing them. He would often target the emotionally vulnerable young men who he came into contact with as suitable candidates for his attentions.'

At much the same time that Father Crowley was using these techniques in various parts of England, Father Gerard Stock, also in the United Kingdom, was doing precisely the same and targeting the same group of potential victims – altar boys. He too was eventually caught and pleaded guilty to thirty-four counts of gross indecency involving sixteen young boys over a twenty-two-year period spanning 1959 to 1981.

Father Adrian McLeish, as parish priest in Gilesgate, Durham, was an avid user of the Internet. When the police raided St Joseph's presbytery they discovered that the priest had built up one of the world's largest collections of Internet pornography. He was also regularly abusing at least four young boys. After police had taken the computers away, Father McLeish, fully aware that he would be going to prison, took a final opportunity to abuse one of his victims. The boy's mother subsequently said, 'It was as if he was having a last fling.' It was further established that McLeish had been using parish funds to pay for his computer pornography. He was sentenced to six years' imprisonment.

Yet another who used his authority to seduce the young was Father Michael Hill. Among the victims of twenty to thirty offences of sexual abuse were two handicapped boys of fourteen and ten. One was confined to a wheelchair and the other had cerebral palsy. They were two of a number of victims who would have been spared their ordeal if the man who is now the Catholic Primate of England, Cardinal Cormac Murphy O'Connor, had been alert on his watch as Bishop of Arundel and Brighton. Less than a year after Murphy O'Connor's promotion to the diocese in 1977, Father Michael Hill came under his control. Hill had been an active paedophile since 1959. One of the features of Hill's later career is the number of times he was shuffled around the diocese. Murphy O'Connor has subsequently gone on record asserting that Hill's removal from Godalming to Heathfield was 'wholly unconnected with any question of child abuse' but was due to 'disagreement and unrest in the parish'. He has yet to specify the causes of the unrest but in late 1980 a number of parishioners from Godalming came to complain to Bishop Murphy O'Connor of the unnaturally close interest Hill was taking in their sons. As one mother recalled, 'I told him what was going on. He said he would deal with it.'

In a classic demonstration of how the secret system operates, Hill was moved to the Parish of Heathfield and sent to a rehabilitation centre run by the Servants of the Paraclete in Gloucestershire. Among other conditions, the centre specialises in treating paedophilia. Cardinal Murphy

O'Connor's subsequent comments regarding his confrontation of Father Hill in 1981 confirmed the truth of the allegations made by the citizens of Godalming. When Hill came to the diocese, his reports carried a health warning that he remained a potential danger to children. Notwithstanding that information, O'Connor allowed him to return to Heathfield parish. By 1983 at least one mother had strongly complained to O'Connor that Father Hill's behaviour towards her two sons was unacceptable and a cause of great concern. Hill received further counselling and this time O'Connor's response to the professional advice that the priest should not be allowed access to children was followed and Father Hill's licence to work in a parish was withdrawn. Then in 1985 the bishop again softened his stance towards Hill. Part of the advice he had received from the medical experts in 1983 was that Hill might be allowed at some point to work in some restricted pastoral role outside the parish.

The Bishop then made an inexcusable decision. He appointed Father Hill as chaplain to Gatwick Airport, which by the time in question, 1985, was known as 'the Leicester Square of Sussex' and 'a magnet for homeless youngsters'. Father Hill took full advantage of his new appointment and committed further sexual attacks upon young boys. When Murphy O'Connor's decision on Father Hill became public knowledge in November 2002, *The Times* newspaper commented that 'the scale of Cardinal Murphy O'Connor's moral blindness is potentially devastating'. Hill was subsequently arrested and found guilty of a number of sexual attacks between 1969 and 1987 including molesting a cerebral palsy sufferer on his way to Lourdes. Father Hill was sentenced to five years' imprisonment.

The Primate of All England has sought to justify his actions with regard to Father Hill on the grounds of a 'genuine ignorance that there was (in the mid to late

1980s) not only among bishops and priests, but also in society at large, including the medical profession, about the compulsive nature of child abuse'. It is a defence without a shred of credibility. In November 2002 Father Hill pleaded guilty to a further string of sexual assaults committed between 1969 and 1987 and was sentenced to a further five years' imprisonment.

The Primate apologised for the 'grave mistake' but his contrition did not extend to resigning his position, despite the many demands from the faithful and from the media that he should leave the national stage. The credibility gap between the Cardinal and his bishops and the ever-shrinking Catholic congregation in England continues to widen. According to the Cardinal's spokesman, the secret deals with victims that have involved the payment of 'hush money' were nothing to do with the Church. 'It does not go near the Church. It is done between solicitor and solicitor.' The spokesman did not say who instructs the solicitor to pay up.

By 1999, as the Catholic Church in England and Wales maintained a silence over the growing convictions of priests for sexual abuse, it had become obvious that paedophilia within the United Kingdom would not be defeated by denying that there was a problem. Twenty-one priests had been convicted in a four-year period. At this crisis point Cardinal Cormac Murphy O'Connor fully acknow-ledged his mistaken handling of Father Hill. Soon afterwards, a full review was established under the chairmanship of Lord Nolan (a former Law Lord and Chairman of the Committee on Standards in Public Life). In April 2001 his report was published, with more than fifty recommendations to protect the potential victims.

It was a positive step and one of its recommendations that was swiftly implemented called for an annual report. Despite numerous instances of clerical sexual abuse over many decades, the Catholic Church of Scotland has not been inclined to follow the example set south of the border. The most important recommendation of the Nolan Report was also rapidly introduced; the creation of a national child protection unit within the Church to 'root out child abusers by vetting clergy, its lay staff and volunteers before they take up new posts'.

The report observed within its executive summary:

> 'Child abuse is a great evil. It can leave deep scars on the victims and their families. It is particularly abhorrent when a child or young person is abused by someone in a position of trust and responsibility. It is most abhorrent when that position of trust is held by a member of the clergy or a lay Catholic worker. The care of children is at the forefront of the teachings of Christ and is, therefore, one of the primary responsibilities of all members of the Church led by their priests and bishops.'

Further, within the summary Lord Nolan and his committee observed a self-evident truth. 'The fact is that should every parish throughout England and Wales follow our recommendations the problem of child abuse would not therefore be eradicated.' It was commendably honest and their final aspiration should have touched a chord with every Roman Catholic within the country:

> 'Our hope is that this report will help to bring about a culture of vigilance where every single adult member of the Church consciously and pro-actively takes responsibility for creating a safe environment for children and young people. Our recommendations are not a substitute for this but we hope they will be an impetus towards such an achievement.'

The Church's commitment to openness certainly struck a chord with the hitherto silent victims. Within the first eighteen months of the new guidelines going into operation, the Church had received nearly 150 further complaints of sex abuse. Another 100 complaints followed in 2004. Archbishop Vincent Nichols of Birmingham welcomed the abuse claims as a clear indication that progress was being made in addressing an historic backlog of abuse.

The Archbishop may have been less enthusiastic when his own archdiocese was obliged to pay out £330,000 to a former altar boy who had been sexually abused by a priest over an eight-year period. The settlement reached in January 2004 was at the time the largest known payout in the United Kingdom. The payout, made days before the case was due to come to the High Court, is a further indication that in England and Wales the times are finally changing, but only in some areas.

In late June 2005, the Birmingham archdiocese was obliged to set the compensation bar twice as high after being ordered by the court to pay over £600,000 (over $1.5 million) to a victim who, as a young boy, had been repeatedly abused by Father Christopher Conlan who had fled the country to Australia where he had died in 1998.

One of the most extraordinary aspects of this scandal had been the dogmatic refusal by the Vatican to accept and acknowledge, until very late in the day, that such abuse was anything more than a local difficulty confined to the United States. As these pages illustrate, the sexual abuse by Catholic priests and religious of children, youths, adolescents and adults knew no frontiers. Pope John Paul II was aware from very early in his reign that this was an issue that he had to address and act on. He failed to address it.

In Austria, a close friend of the Pope's, Cardinal Hans Hermann Groer, was forced after a protracted struggle to resign following allegations of repeatedly abusing students

at an all-male Catholic school. Groer rejected the allegations. In Switzerland, Bishop Hansjörg Vogel of Basel
resigned after admitting he had impregnated a woman
following his promotion to the hierarchy in the previous
year. Standing behind every bishop referred to above is
the same pattern of institutional abuse, the same range
of paedophiliac sexual abuses by priests. Appalling abuse
by the Christian Brothers has been matched by cruelty from
the Poor Sisters of Nazareth or the Daughters of Charity of
St Vincent de Paul or the Sisters of Mercy. For more than
100 years there were Nazareth homes all over the United
Kingdom, Australia, South Africa, the United States and
Ireland.

From the mid-nineteenth century to recent times 'Nazareth homes' cared for the young and the old. The orphanages
were run by nuns from the order of the Sisters of Mercy.
Violent degradation and thrashings were a daily event. The
children woke up to the screams of other children and to the
familiar sound of the strap. In 1965 Helen Cusiter was eight
years of age when her mother disappeared and she was
taken, along with her five brothers, to the Nazareth House
in Aberdeen. In 2004 at the age of forty-seven, after a
chance meeting with one of her childhood tormentors,
Helen became one of over five hundred former residents
to bring an action against the Sisters. Her recall of what she
had endured was corroborated by other former inmates
who had not met for a lifetime. It included a particular
incident with Sister Alphonso who had come looking for
her while Helen had been playing on the swings.

> 'She took me off by the hair, twisted me round and
> threw me against the church wall. She broke all my
> front teeth, my face was a mashed mess, the other kids
> were all screaming.' Helen Howie, one of those
> screaming children, remembers the blood pouring

from Helen's face: 'Sister Alphonso didn't use leather straps, she used her fists, she had such strength.' When the dentist queried the extensive bruising on the eight year old's face he was told, 'She fell.'

Sister Aphonso was convicted on four charges of cruel and unnatural treatment. Because of her age she was merely admonished rather than imprisoned. There are all too many similar testimonies from hundreds of damaged people. Many sought not compensation but just the opportunity of being heard, of having the pain they still felt acknowledged.

The Poor Sisters are no longer poor. They have approaching £200 million in their bank and have eventually dropped the 'Poor' from their title. There is now an international campaign to bring the Order to the bar of justice. It will be an uphill struggle with the insurance companies combining with a number of the bishops to ward off the attack.

Many bishops are still in denial about the enormity and extent of clerical sexual abuse over the past forty to fifty years. They still consider it as a 'problem' that should be dealt with in-house – without publicity or criminal charges. In January 2003 the Irish commission created to enquire into child abuse publicly complained that 'the Government and most religious orders are obstructing our work'. The Commission was investigating Church-run institutions to which the Irish Government sent 'problem' children and orphans. As in Canada, in Ireland much had been covered up. There were fifty-two 'industrial schools' in the mid-twentieth century where physical and sexual abuse were rife. An industrial school functioned as an early type of reform centre or Borstal. They were devised as 'Means for Decreasing Juvenile Crime'. Often the only 'crime' was that the child had been orphaned or abandoned. In theory, apart from teaching the ordinary elementary subjects, the children also were taught a trade. The varying circumstances made no difference to the treatment meted out. Whether those entrusted with the children were Christian Brothers, Daughters of Charity or Poor Sisters of Nazareth the viciousness of the various religious orders had a disturbing uniformity. Since 1985 more than 4,000 survivors of a *child slave labour regime* have sought compensation from the Irish Catholic Church. One who is beyond winning any compensation is Willie Delaney.

In 1966 at the age of nine, Willie was the oldest of ten children, living in a caravan without sanitation or running water. It was his responsibility to help to feed the family. His father, a tinsmith confronting a shrinking market with the advent of long-life kitchen utensils, needed all the help he could get. Willie was caught stealing piglets and sentenced to six years in Letterfrack, an industrial school in the west of Ireland, described by survivors as 'a hell on earth'. Inmates suffered physical, mental and sexual abuse. Willie was treated brutally. In 1970, by now thirteen, a few days before he was due home for a precious two-week holiday, Willie was continuously beaten about the head. Survivors have recently testified that one of the Christian Brothers was continuously beating Willie's head with a bunch of keys; others remember him using a pole. At home Willie complained of severe headaches, then he suffered a fit, went into a coma and died. Doctors at St Luke's Hospital in Kilkenny said he had died of meningitis. His father was certain his death was linked with the treatment he had suffered from the Christian Brothers.

In April 2001 Willie's body was exhumed and subjected to a post-mortem. It was determined that he had died from natural causes but Willie's death and its aftermath had given a further thirty former inmates the courage to come forward and lay complaints against Christian Brothers and lay staff. The eventual number of complaints rose to 140. Twenty-nine Christian Brothers and lay staff were identified as alleged abusers. Forty-eight priests and Christian brothers had already been convicted of abusing, physically and sexually, children in their care.

In an unrelated case in Ireland a few months before the exhumation of Willie Delaney, a former Franciscan Brother, Robert Keoghan, pleaded guilty to eight charges of indecently assaulting eight boys aged between nine and sixteen on various dates between 1969 and 1972. Before sentencing Keoghan, who was already serving an eighteen-month prison sentence for two similar crimes, the court heard that when Keoghan had gone to confess these offences he had been sexually abused by his confessor, a Franciscan priest. Keoghan was sentenced to a further two years' imprisonment.

As the dam was breached worldwide, it was striking how frequently the activities of the paedophiliac priests could be traced back twenty, thirty or even forty years earlier. It is inconceivable that just one particular generation of priests who took Holy Orders in the late 1950s and the 1960s should be any more or less inclined to paedophilia than the generation before or the generation after. Traditionalists have blamed the rise in abuse on the reforms of Vatican Council II, but they have yet to reveal the cause of the clerical paedophilia that predates the mid-1960s. One is left with the nightmare possibility that but for the case of Father Gauthe, the secret system would still be functioning efficiently, with just as many new victims being abused. Yet even after 1985, there were attempts to keep the old order. In the early years of the new century, Hong Kong police were investigating clerical crimes. They discovered that the secret system was still alive and fully operational in May 2002. Police Superintendent Shirley Chu, who was investigating eight abuse cases, publicly complained that the

Catholic Church was refusing to hand over written confessions by a number of priests made during an internal Church investigation. Chu's response echoed that of judges, police officers and district attorneys around the world: 'It seems that the Church has been protecting its reputation and priests rather than the victims.'

The Catholic hierarchy in the Philippines were also forced to apologise to victims. In September 2000, thirty-four priests and a number of bishops were suspended as the full extent of clerical sex abuse began to be known publicly. Unlike in many other countries, the majority of cases involved the sexual abuse of women. It was subsequently revealed that in New Zealand in early 1991 six Roman Catholic dioceses had confirmed thirty-eight cases of sexual abuse by priests and brothers, within two years of a complaints procedure being set up: a great many more were in the pipeline including complaints of abuse that reached back fifty years to the 1940s. For most of that period the Catholic population of New Zealand was less than 500,000, with only around 500 priests: the confirmed cases indicated a historic average of some 7 per cent of priests being sex abusers.

Commenting on the figures, Lyndsay Freer, the National Director of Catholic Communications, displayed the national gift for understatement: 'There was a tendency in the past to protect the institution or the profession.' Then, singing from the same hymn sheet as the rest of the Catholic Church, Freer attempted to defend the indefensible.

'The recidivist nature of psychosexual dysfunction or paedophilia was not understood, and it was thought that if a person admitted guilt, confessed it, and was given absolution in the sacrament in Confession . . . rehabilitation and forgiveness was possible.'

In Australia, Cardinal Pell was obliged to admit that the Church had not relied on mere Christian forgiveness on the part of the victim. Many thousands of dollars of hush money had been paid to those who had suffered sexual abuse. Less than two weeks later the Roman Catholic Order the St John of God Brothers revealed that they had reached an out-of-court settlement with lawyers representing twenty-four mentally handicapped men who had been sexually abused by up to twenty Brothers while in their care. The amount to be paid was 2.1 million US dollars and is believed to be the largest such settlement in Australian history. Finding courage in the example set by the mentally handicapped victims, a further 157 alleged victims came forward. Meanwhile the head of the Church in South Africa admitted that about a dozen priests had been accused of sexually abusing children 'many years ago'. Demonstrably, the secret system had worked well in all of these countries.

In Brazil, the world's largest predominantly Roman Catholic country, Church officials admitted there was a paedophilia problem among the clergy. Bishop Angelico Sandalo Bernardino in an extraordinary attempt at justification observed, 'The problem of sexual appetite is one that afflicts every human being.'

In Holland, the pragmatic Dutch Church attempted an unusual and highly dubious strategy in secret negotiations with its insurers. They demanded that an additional clause covering sexual abuse compensation be inserted in their policies. They further demanded that it be applied *retrospectively* to cover the past decades. Both demands were rejected.

A similar contretemps occurred in Ireland. It transpired that the insurance cover for the Irish Church that included the aspect of sexual abuse had first been taken out by the Irish Bishops' Conference between 1987 and 1990, a period when the bishops were still using the secret system and busily moving offending priests from parish to parish. In the words of the bishops' spokesman, Father Martin Clarke, the cover 'offered only modest coverage at low premiums'. Once a wave of child abuse scandals began engulfing the Irish Church in 1994, the insurance policies proved 'ambiguous and uncertain', a discovery with regard to insurance policies that is not unique to the Catholic Church. Insurance companies all over the world pushed the panic button overnight; premiums rose to anything between 30 per cent and 130 per cent for far less coverage.

Following the example set by the Church in England and Wales, the Irish Bishops' Conference commissioned an independent study of child abuse by the Catholic clergy in Ireland. It was carried out by the Royal College of Surgeons in Ireland and a press release, but not the report itself, was made public in December 2003 on behalf of the Irish Bishops. Having noted that 'over half' of the report's recommendations were already being followed, Bishop John McAreavey then pointed to the report's 'acknowledgement that when dealing with abusers in the past, bishops followed, in good faith, the best psychiatric advice available at the time'. This acknowledgement flies in the face of decades of lies, cover-ups, evasions and wilful disregard of the victims. He continued: 'Clearly in relation to clerical sexual abuse we failed many young people over too long a period.'

One of the authors of the report, Professor Hannah McGee, saw her own conclusions rather differently. 'The occurrence, and more importantly the mismanagement, of clerical child abuse, represents a loss throughout Irish society rather than an isolated problem for an unfortunate few.'

Bishop McAreavey did have the good grace to apologise

publicly for the wrongs of the past and to make a commitment to improve 'upon our existing policies'. The undertaking would have carried greater conviction if the bishops
had not sought to shift the burden of blame on to the
shoulders of consultant psychiatrists.

At the time of the Royal College of Surgeons' report,
another enquiry, this time into alleged sexual abuse of
children in the diocese of Ferns in Ireland, was already
one year into what would eventually become a three-year
investigation. The Commission identified over 100 allegations of sexual abuse by twenty-one priests between
1962 and 2002. Their report, published in October
2005, confirmed that sexual abuse was widespread over
many years in Ferns. Ten of the accused priests were dead,
two were convicted and the remainder were 'not in active
ministry'. Quite why that gave them immunity from
prosecution has yet to be explained.

The Catholic Church in Ireland insists that under Canon
Law sexually abusing clerics are immune from criminal
prosecution unless that immunity is lifted by either the
bishop or by Rome. Far too many of the hierarchy in
Ireland still cling to a Supreme Court judgement of 1925
when the highest court in Ireland accepted the right of the
Bishop of Kerry to remove a parish priest from West Cork
against the priest's wishes. That judgement is now being
used by Irish bishops to thwart natural justice as the Church
clings to a fantasy that abusing a child is not a criminal
offence but a moral issue.

In April 2003, twenty-five years after the Gauthe case,
Vatican officials sat with psychologists and therapists
behind locked doors while they held a conference on the
sexual abuse of children. Still the desire not to 'embarrass
Holy Mother Church' persisted – although the image of the
Church already lay in shreds.

In France, the secret system was preserved until the

twenty-first century. In January 2000, Abbot Jean-Lucien Maurel was sentenced to ten years' imprisonment for raping and sexually abusing three boys aged between ten and thirteen. Maurel was seventy-one at the time of his trial and sixty-seven at the time of the attacks. The boys were pupils at the school where the Abbot was headmaster. Between fifteen and twenty other French Catholic clergy were also under investigation for alleged sex abuses.

A year later in 2001, a French bishop, Pierre Pican of Bayeux-Lisieux, was convicted of covering up the sexual abuses of one of his priests. He said, 'It is unfortunate that this verdict has limited the Catholic priest's right to keep professional secrets.' In truth it had nothing to do with the sanctity of the confessional and everything to do with what is still a very widely held view within the Catholic Church that her priests and bishops are above the law. The abuser in question, Father René Bissey, is now serving an eighteen-year prison sentence; his bishop got a three-month suspended prison sentence.

The attitude of Bishop Pican is not unique: in fact it is the norm. In 2002, the Chairman of the German Bishops' Conference, Cardinal Lehmann, was asked by *Der Spiegel*,

'When cases are suspected, are the judicial authorities called in?' He responded, 'This is not our task. The authorities involve themselves . . . in clear-cut cases – we ourselves are often in the dark – we motivate the culprit to self-denunciation. That is better for everybody. In addition, we undertake our own preliminary investigations; that is dictated by Canon Law. If there is enough evidence the relevant person is suspended from office. But that is a matter for individual dioceses. The Bishops' Conference is not responsible for such matters.'

Pressed on the need for 'binding rules' that would apply to all dioceses with regard to their dealings with paedophile priests, Cardinal Lehmann disagreed:

> 'We have large dioceses where over decades they have accumulated their own experience as to how to handle these offences and they do not just want to hand the matter over to a higher authority.'

That accumulated experience represents the ability to cover and conceal the great majority of paedophile cases that threaten to come to light in Germany. Diligent application of the secret system ensures that exposure of paedophile priests on the scale of the United States scandal will not happen in Germany or other European countries.

The Catholic psychotherapist Wunibald Müller, a man with decades of experience in the treatment of priests with psychological and psychiatric problems, has estimated that there is a minimum of 2 per cent of all priests in Germany with a predisposition to paedophilia, giving a national figure of between 250 and 300. Paedophiles are invariably serial offenders and therefore the number of children at very real risk in Germany today, even by the most conservative of estimates, is somewhere between 5,000 and 10,000. The actual figure is undoubtedly much higher. Müller's estimate was based on the evidence that has been made available to him through clinical study of the general German population. But the extraordinary efficiency of the German application of the secret system has for decades dramatically suppressed the abnormal incidence of sexual abuse among the clerical population. Consequently Müller's estimates are only around half of comparable estimates for other countries, notably the USA. His figure is disturbingly low.

In the United States during the fifteen years after the Gauthe case of 1985/86, over 1,200 paedophile priests were exposed. In view of the fact that there have continued to be weekly if not daily exposures, new civil claims and continuous fresh allegations, the actual total continues to move in the United States inexorably towards 3,000 paedophiles or 5 per cent of the Roman Catholic priesthood. Even those estimates may prove to be far too low when more exhaustive research has been completed. If the evidence from the Indiana diocese of Lafayette was to be replicated across the United States, all of the previous estimates would have to be rewritten. In a diocese of just seventy-five active priests, by early 1997 it had been established that at least 16 per cent were guilty of a wide range of sexual abuses.

It should be remembered that these figures were not reached against a background of an open, transparent Church but one which used every delaying tactic that it could dream up with the help of its lawyers and insurers, a Church where paedophile bishops protected paedophile priests with a bodyguard of deceit. One example was Bishop J. Keith Symons of Palm Beach, who compiled the 'professional psychiatric evaluations that at the time clearly demonstrated the fitness of Rev. Rocco D'Angelo to serve as a priest'.

At the time of these evaluations both the bishop and the priest were sexually abusing young boys. After complaints from the parents of the victims were made to the archdiocese of Miami in the 1960s the parents had been promised that D'Angelo would be kept from children. The secret system was applied and D'Angelo was transferred to the Tampa area where he worked for more than two decades while continuing to molest young boys, one of them in 1987, more than twenty-five years after the Church had given an undertaking that it had never intended to honour.

Father D'Angelo took early retirement in 1993 after his sexual activities became public knowledge. Bishop Symons followed him into early retirement in June 1997 after admitting that he had sexually molested five boys more than three decades earlier. His 'new broom' replacement was Bishop Anthony O'Connell. Four years later there was need of another new broom, as Bishop O'Connell was forced to resign in March 2002 after revelations about his sexual activities with young men who had been under his supervision as rector of a Missouri seminary.

In Boston, an archdiocese that serves a Catholic population of over two million, the Church has been brought to its knees financially. The faith of many has been shattered by an endless stream of clerical sex abuse scandals. In 1992 Cardinal Bernard F. Law of Boston called down 'the power of God' on the news media after their coverage of the activities of the Rev. James R. Porter. A quick résumé of Porter's life leaves one marvelling that the Cardinal went to the barricades for him.

In 1953, aged eighteen, Porter molested a thirteen-year-old boy in a playground in his hometown of Revere, Massachusetts. In the later 1950s Porter, then a seminarian, worked during the summers at the Cathedral Camp in East Freetown, Massachusetts. He molested children at virtually every opportunity and was reported by a victim to another worker-priest. No action was taken and back in Revere, Porter sexually molested numerous local children. In 1960 Porter received his first assignment as a priest – at a kindergarten to eighth grade school, St Mary's Church and Elementary in North Attleborough. During a two-year period Father Porter sexually assaulted scores of children aged between six and fourteen.

Decades later, 68 of these victims recounted their experiences to psychologist James Daignault. 'The first time I remember was when I was eleven,' said Ms Burns. 'I heard someone crying in the school bathroom.' When she went in to see who it was she found Father Porter raping a six-year-old girl. 'I tried to stop him, but he grabbed me and sodomised me. He was absolutely violent. He told me that he was stronger than me and that he had the power of God.'

Stephen Johnson also told his experiences to Daignault:

'When I would scream, he would put his hand over my mouth so no one would hear me. James Porter sexually assaulted me countless times, and each time he would chastise me by saying that what I had done was very bad and that God would punish me if I told anyone.'

Stephen, who was an altar boy at Porter's North Attleborough Church, expressed a sentiment that accurately describes not only his own trauma but that of countless victims of paedophile priests.

'Shame and guilt became the foundation of my being.'

In 1962 when a group of parents and relatives of some of the victims went as a deputation to see pastor Father Booth and Father Annunziato of St Mary's Church to complain and demand action, Father Booth responded, 'He is already receiving treatment. What are you trying to do? Crucify him?' Diocesan records released in 1992 revealed that as of 1962 Bishop Connolly's office had details of over thirty boys who had been abused by Father Porter to whom the secret system was applied again and again. He was transferred to Fall River, some twenty-five miles away from North Attleborough. He continued to abuse children, and after more complaints he was transferred to New Bedford, fifteen miles from Fall River. The priests were told by the Diocesan Office to 'watch Father Porter' because he has 'a problem with little boys'. The watching was inadequate, and more sexual abuse of children by Father Porter was followed by a complaint to the New Hampshire police, who simply escorted Father Porter over the state line and then released him.

In 1967 after yet more attacks on children, the Diocesan Office at Fall River sent Porter for treatment to the rehabilitation centre run by the Servants of the Paraclete at Jemez Springs, New Mexico. After a period of treatment he was allowed to go out on a trial basis to say mass at churches in New Mexico and Texas and also work as chaplain at a children's hospital, where he sexually abused a patient confined in a full body cast. The rehabilitation centre records for the period noted that Father Porter was once again indulging in 'his old failings'. Uncured, Porter was given a letter of recommendation by the Paraclete Centre to the parish of Bemidji in Minnesota. Between 1969 and 1970 while at the parish Father Porter sexually abused a further twenty to thirty children. Again he was caught.

Eventually in 1973 Porter made a written application to Pope Paul VI to be allowed to leave the priesthood. In his letter he told the Pope that he had molested a large number of children in five different states. His papal dispensation was granted on 5 January 1974. Two years later Porter married and subsequently fathered several children. Despite this external normality, he was still an active paedophile and sexually molested a number of local boys in the area of Minnesota where he was then living. In 1984 he molested a teenage female babysitter caring for his four children. In 1987 he molested her fifteen-year-old sister. In 1989 Porter was questioned in connection with the disappearance of an eleven-year-old boy, Jacob Wetterling. During interrogation by FBI officers he admitted that while a Catholic priest he had sexually abused and molested at least thirty to forty children. The FBI took no action.

In 1992 what had begun as a one-man crusade by Frank

Fitzpatrick, a former child victim of Father Porter, culminated in a TV programme in which eight victims told of the
abuses he had perpetrated upon them many years earlier.
The programme inspired yet more victims to come forward,
which in turn triggered yet more publicity. It was this
exposure that so angered Cardinal Law that he called down
'the power of God' on the news media.

Notwithstanding the Cardinal's efforts to suppress the
truth, Porter was indicted the same year in Massachusetts
for molesting twenty-eight children, offences that were still
within the statute of limitations. The same day he was also
indicted in Minnesota for the molestation of his babysitter.
Subsequently he was found guilty of the latter offence and
sentenced to six months' imprisonment. In 1993, confronted with forty-one counts of indecent assault, unnatural
acts and sodomy involving twenty-eight of his victims, the
former priest made a plea-bargained deal and was sentenced to eighteen to twenty years' imprisonment. By that
time, ninety-nine of his victims had come forward from the
three parishes. The number is now approaching 150 and
continues to increase. The Catholic Church has paid out
between $5 million and $10 million in various settlements
to Porter's victims.

Around this time an Italian Cardinal described the child
abuse scandal to me as a 'curious American hysteria that
would soon wither and die away'. His attitude was common in the Vatican. Yet it was exploded by further scandalous revelations as the 1990s progressed. In July 1997 a
Texas jury awarded eleven former altar boys $119.6 mil-
lion. It was the largest known settlement in a clergy sexual
molestation case in the United States. Only ten of the
plaintiffs were still able to derive any benefit from the
award: the other, Jay Lemberger, shot himself at the age
of twenty-one. The jury found that the Dallas Catholic
Diocese and the sexual abuse by the defendant Father

Rudolph Kos were the 'proximate cause' of his suicide. Kos had sexually abused around fifty boys between 1981 and 1992. One of the victims testified that the priest abused him over a four-year period beginning when he was ten. Another told the jury he was sexually abused by Kos over 350 times.

The size of the award stunned the Catholic Church. It brought nearer the billion-dollar estimate of potential financial loss made twelve years earlier by Father Doyle and his colleagues, once dismissed as wildly fanciful. The diocesan lawyers and the lawyers representing two insurance companies, Lloyds of London and Interstate Fire and Casualty went to war. After a range of tactics that included endless stalling and countless negotiations they eventually succeeded in pushing the settlement down to $30 million but alarm bells were ringing in many an archbishop's residence, nowhere more loudly than in Boston.

The man ringing the bell of Cardinal Law's residence was John Geoghan, ordained a priest in 1962 and defrocked with the Pope's authority by Cardinal Law in 1998. Over thirty-one years Geoghan had served in six parishes in the Boston area leaving human wreckage behind him in every one. Successive bishops had operated the secret system and moved the compulsive paedophile around, spreading his damage far and wide. By the time he had been stripped of his priesthood, the archdiocese had settled twelve civil lawsuits against Geoghan, paying at least fifty victims a total of around $10 million. But fifty victims in thirty years was far from the final tally for Father Geoghan and those who had knowingly protected him.

Cardinal Law was the last in a long line to accord Geoghan facilities that enabled him to continue his paedophilia activities. Law was not, unfortunately, unique. The much beloved Cardinal of Chicago, Joseph Bernadin, and

the majority of cardinals, archbishops and bishops functioning in the United States over the entire second half of the
twentieth century also operated the secret system. It took
until January 2002 before the state succeeded in bringing
criminal proceedings against the man whose protectors
reached back far beyond Cardinal Cody. As Geoghan's
career as a serial sex abuser flowered so did the careers of
those who had assisted him. Cardinal Humberto Medeiros
had protected Father Porter as a Monsignor. As a Cardinal,
controlling the entire archdiocese, he protected Geoghan.
Bishops Daily, Banks, McCormack and Murphy had also in
the past protected Father Geoghan in a growing number of
dioceses before they moved on with promotions. Archbishop Alfred Hughes of New Orleans was another who
looked out for Geoghan in earlier times.

In January 2002 the former priest was found guilty of
sexually molesting a ten-year-old boy and sentenced to eight
to ten years of imprisonment. Additional criminal charges
were scheduled to be heard at later dates. An additional
eighty-six victims were now free to bring civil cases against
Geoghan and the archdiocese of Boston. They sought
damages against Cardinal Bernard Law. The case concen-
trated the cardinal's mind wonderfully. By May, Law had
agreed a settlement with the eighty-six victims of $30
million. The cardinal's finance council were acutely aware
that many other victims of paedophile priests were watching developments with their lawyers. They baulked at the
settlement figure and the cardinal's lawyers were sent back
to the negotiating table.

The Geoghan trial had triggered an extraordinary new
wave of claims across the United States. By April 2002, 177
priests had been removed in twenty-eight states. By June
more than 300 civil law suits alleging clerical sexual abuse
had been filed in sixteen states. Lawyers confirmed that a
further 250 cases were being informally mediated between

dioceses and accusers. Attorneys estimated that it would take two to three years to resolve the cases already filed and new cases were emerging virtually every day. By June the number of priests who had either been dismissed or resigned since January had risen to 250. Every prediction that Father Doyle, Father Peterson and Ray Mouton had made within their advisory Manual in 1985 had come to pass.

By mid-April 2002 many observers considered that Cardinal Law's position as head of the Boston archdiocese was untenable. The Geoghan scandal had still to be resolved and further shocking revelations were imminent, including the identities of other paedophile priests protected by the cardinal and his bishops. The Boston judges were beginning to exercise their power and demand that the archdiocese hand over the files on two of these, Fathers Mahan and Shanley. Mahan's activities allegedly covered a period from 1962 to his removal from the priesthood in 1998. Shanley was accused of crimes that ranged from paedophilia and public advocacy of sexual intercourse between men and boys to teaching youngsters how to shoot up with heroin.

Cardinal Law's officials dug in and were applying a range of delaying tactics to avoid handing over the incriminating files but the clock was showing 'time' everywhere but within the Vatican. In mid-April 2002 Cardinal Law secretly travelled to Rome. For a man accustomed to arrivals and departures with the full pomp and ceremony that befitted a Prince of the Roman Catholic Church, it was a sobering experience to be smuggled out of his own residence and hustled through Logan airport like a fugitive from justice.

The Cardinal and the Pope were close friends but there was a gulf of perception between them during the meeting. Bernard Law's exposure to the media coverage, the rising tide of protests, not only from the Catholic in the street but from people within the Boston hierarchy, could not be

ignored. The calls for his resignation had been growing by
the day. Law had refused for more than two months to talk
to the news media; he did not consider himself accountable
either to the public at large or to his Catholic flock. He was
answerable to the Pope and none other. Technically the
Cardinal's position was correct but neither the news media
nor ordinary Catholics pay much attention to Canon Law.
In the preceding months the Cardinal had attempted to win
the day by hiring public relations consultants and addressing the scandal from his pulpit. As for responsibility, the
Cardinal had confined himself to apologising twice and
simultaneously blaming 'inadequate medical advice',
'inadequate record keeping of erring priests' and 'an excessive media focus on clergy sexual abuse'.

Throughout the entire seventeen years since the Gauthe
case, neither the Pope nor his senior advisors had confronted the cancer of paedophilia within the Catholic
Church. It was an extraordinary omission and a devastating failure with far-reaching consequences. At his meetings
Cardinal Law attempted to bring the Vatican up to date
with developments within the Boston archdiocese. When
Archbishop Marcinkus had come complaining about the
drubbing he was getting over his mismanagement of the
Vatican Bank, the Pope had airily dismissed the matter as
being something to be ignored. For many of the preceding
seventeen years he had adopted much the same attitude to
the sexual abuses being perpetrated by his priests, bishops
and religious. Even now with the Boston Cardinal sitting
in front of him recounting the Goeghan case, the Shanley
case, the Porter case and others, the Pope was inclined to
blame influences outside the clergy. When the Cardinal
offered to resign the Pope waved the offer away. 'Your
place is at the head of the Archdiocese.' And sent him back
to Boston.

The Pope had been convinced for a long time that 'this

problem' was unique to the United States and that it would burn itself out. He had chosen to ignore a global reality and his continuing inaction had ensured a constantly deteriorating situation that no amount of media messaging could solve. Perhaps inevitably, the Church decided on a press relations exercise. The Boston cardinal's deep aversion to the media, which he largely blamed for the crisis, ensured that he would continue to treat them with contempt. No one had been advised he was going to Rome and no one was going to get to interview him now he was back in Boston. He elected to make a press statement. Having in the past week offered his resignation to the papal nuncio in Washington and to the Pope in Rome and having been told to ignore his critics, he said, 'I return home encouraged in my efforts to provide the strongest possible leadership in ensuring, as far as is humanly possible, that no child is ever abused again by a priest of this archdiocese.'

It was an admirable statement but it was obvious that, rather than reach out to his flock of over two million souls through every available news outlet, the cardinal with the Pope's approval had chosen an esoteric form of communication.

'It is my intent to address at length the record of the archdiocese's handling of these cases by reviewing the past in as systematic and comprehensive a way as possible, so that the legitimate questions which have been raised might be answered. The facilities of Boston Catholic Television and *The Pilot* will assist in making this record available.'

He deemed only a minority channel and the parish magazine competent to carry the information on a story with national and international ramifications. As an example of how to lose friends and alienate people it was definitive.

The *Boston Globe and Mail* carried Cardinal Law's statement as well as the results of its most recent poll on the scandal. This showed that 65 per cent thought Law should leave his job, 71 per cent thought the cardinal had done a poor job handling the various instances of sexual abuse of children by priests and 53 per cent said they had now lost confidence in the Catholic Church as an institution because of the scandal. The survey polled 800 Catholic adults. Meanwhile, lawyers redoubled their efforts to obtain archdiocesan records on Father Shanley and other paedophiles and judges were insisting that Cardinal Law make a formal deposition and provide the archdiocesan files on Father Geoghan.

The Vatican then announced that the Pope had summoned every American Cardinal to Rome. Many observers in the United States saw this as a positive step, a sign that Pope John Paul II was finally going to get a grip on the most serious crisis to confront his papacy since the Banco Ambrosiano crash. The cynics within the City State nodded and smiled. They fully agreed with the comments of Cardinal Dario Castrillón Hoyos, Head of the Vatican Congregation of the Clergy, who only three weeks earlier dismissed the media preoccupation in the United States scandal. Hoyos believed that the Holy Father's agenda allowed no time for concerns over the abuse of children. He airily declared, 'The Pope is worried about peace in the world.'

From 1978 until April 2002 the Pope had deliberately and studiously avoided any public references to the global epidemic of sexual abuse by his priests and members of Catholic orders, apart from a few oblique comments. He had talked in March 2002 of 'a dark shadow of suspicion' that had been cast over priests 'by some of our brothers who have betrayed the grace of ordination' and have succumbed to the 'most grievous forms of the mystery of evil at work in the world'. He could not quite bring himself to utter the word paedophilia.

Equally silent was the Prefect of the Congregation for the Doctrine of the Faith – the CDF – Cardinal Ratzinger. What made his failure to go public on the worldwide scandal of clerical sexual abuse inexplicable was the fact that at least since June 1988 by direct command of Pope John Paul II the CDF was duly authorised to investigate and sit in judgement on a range of clerical sexual abuse including 'violation against the sixth commandment of the Decalogue committed by a cleric with a minor below the age of eighteen years'.

The one significant exception to the papal silence was a curious paragraph hidden away in a 120-page document that summed up the themes of a Synod of Bishops of Oceania in the Vatican in 1998.

'Sexual abuse by some clergy and religious has caused great suffering and spiritual harm to the victims. It has been very damaging in the life of the Church and has become an obstacle to the proclamation of the Gospel. The Synod fathers condemned all sexual abuse and forms of abuse of power both within the Church and in society as a whole.'

Although the speech dates from 1998 no one within the Vatican saw fit to make it available to the public until it was put on the Internet on 22 November 2001. The comments were widely understood within the Vatican as referring not to child abuse but to another aspect of clerical and religious sexual abuse, one that is examined later within this section.

Just three days before the US cardinals were due to arrive at the Vatican, the Pope delivered a strong reaffirmation of the importance of priestly celibacy. His remarks were seen as cutting the ground away from under the feet of some of the US cardinals who had gone on record a week earlier declaring that the entire issue of celibacy should be re-examined. Many believed that the imposition of celibacy was directly linked to a significant proportion of the clerical sexual abuse cases. The Pope was not prepared even to discuss this idea. His eulogy on priestly celibacy was given in the presence of the visiting Nigerian bishops, who interpreted the comments to refer to the fact that in Africa many priests were indulging in regular sexual relationships with women.

The image of the Pope seated on a slightly raised dais with twelve American cardinals ranged out in a long horse-shoe before him and two senior members of the Curia standing behind him stays in the memory. The cameras had been allowed in briefly to record part of the Pope's welcoming speech and concluding remarks. This was intended as the first stage in the Vatican's press relations exercise. The speech did indeed contain a number of headline-grabbing phrases:

'The abuse which has caused this crisis is by every standard wrong and rightly considered a crime by society; it is also an appalling sin in the eyes of God. To the victims and their families, wherever they may be, I express my profound sense of solidarity and concern . . . People need to know that there is no place in the priesthood and religious life for those who would harm the young . . .'
'. . . Because of the great harm done by some priests and religious, the Church herself is viewed with dis-trust, and many are offended at the way the Church leaders are perceived to have acted in this matter . . . The abuse of the young is a grave symptom of a crisis affecting not only the Church but society as a whole.'

Defending the Catholic Church in America, the Pope talked of how it had always promoted human and Christian values with 'great vigour and generosity, in a way that has helped to consolidate all that is noble in the American people'. That was a highly debatable proposition, as was his image of the Church in the United States and in the wider world: 'A great work of art may be blemished, but its beauty remains; and this is a truth which any intellectually honest critic will recognise.'

While the cardinals sat within the Vatican discussing the child abuse scandal, back in Philadelphia the District Attorney announced a grand jury investigation into sexual abuse claims against thirty-five local priests. The alleged abuse ranged over the previous fifty years. Opinion polls in the *Washington Post* and ABC News indicated that 75 per cent of Americans believed the Church's image to be deeply tarnished.

The meeting concluded with the Pope and his American cardinals at one on the need to weed out paedophile priests with a policy of zero tolerance. The cardinals were given the express task of creating guidelines to deal with the crisis that would be presented to the US Conference of Catholic Bishops in June in Dallas. The American cardinals then gave a press conference and responded to questions from the huge crowd of reporters. The main item on the agenda for the news media was whether or not Cardinal Law had resigned. The smart money was betting that Law's time as head of the Boston archdiocese was over. Not for the first time the smart money was wrong.

Of the twelve cardinals only three attended the press conference: the missing nine included Cardinal Law who had not resigned. Though the majority of his colleagues had wanted him to fall on his sword, the Pope had declined to let him. In considerable disarray, the cardinals and their camp followers returned to the USA.

The cardinals' evident divisions were nothing compared with the Pope's advisors. Many of them still believed that this was an American problem. They were also deeply divided about the Pope's apparent commitment to zero tolerance. The Pope's forthright denunciation of clerical and religious sexual abuse in April 2002 had been preceded by an almost complete denial of the scandal. Firm action taken early in his papacy would not have wiped out the obscenities perpetrated before October 1978 but through transparency and honest confrontation, and a rapid abolition of the secret system, John Paul II would have saved the Church much grief and, more importantly, he would have prevented untold suffering and pain for the victims yet to come. By also reaching out with counselling, compensation and compassion to those already abused, the Church could have begun their healing nearly thirty years earlier. For some it can now never begin.

Celebrating World Youth Day in Denver, Colorado, in 1993 the Pope had alluded to the scandal which had already convulsed America for nearly ten years. He told a packed audience that he shared the concerns of US bishops for the 'pain and suffering caused by some priests' sins'. He did not mention the pain and suffering caused by the bishops through the operation of the secret system, nor did he endorse any specific punishments for the offenders. The suffering of the victims would be eased 'by prayer'. The cause of the abuse scandals in the USA was a 'widespread false morality . . . America needs much prayer lest it loses its soul'. The issues of birth control and abortion 'have caused strains between US Catholics and the Vatican . . . polar-isation and destructive criticism have no place within the Church'. A few weeks later the Vatican released a statement repeating their claim that clergy sexual abuse was an American and Canadian problem.

Among those listening to the Pope in Denver were a number of the victims of this 'North American' problem.

One was Tom Economus, a former altar boy who had been raped and regularly abused by family friend and mentor Father Don Murray. During my research for this part I interviewed Tom Economus and he recounted in detail how Murray had manipulated and used him. He also recounted how when he subsequently sought counselling, the priest he turned to for help attempted to rape him.

Father Murray had been an 'out-of-control alcoholic', the counsellor 'was just out of any control'. Economus became a member of the breakaway Independent Catholic Church and was ordained a priest. Because of his experiences Economus became a powerful advocate for the victims of clergy abuse. He led efforts to expose perpetrators and demanded accountability from religious leaders. He also became President of Linkup, a support group for clergy abuse victims of all faiths.

I asked him about his attendance in Denver. He replied,

'It was obvious to me by the early 1990s that neither the Vatican nor the Pope were going anywhere with the issue of clergy sexual abuse. World Youth Day in Denver, when the Pope was going to pray with more than 150,000 young people, seemed a good place to make a point. We were demonstrating on behalf of the victims. I'd got together getting on for 3,000 letters from victims and their families. I presented them to the Vatican security staff to be given to the Pope. They refused to take them. Threw them on the ground. I brought them back to this office and sent them to the Vatican. I never had a response.'

Father Economus observed, 'About two months later the Mount Cashel scandal erupted in Newfoundland. Within the year twenty-eight countries were engulfed in the "North American" problem.' In March 2002 Tom Economus, aged forty-six, died of cancer at his Chicago home. Father Economus is one of a long line of victims ignored by the Vatican and the Pope.

Press relations exercises for the Pope have ranged from talking to Bono, the lead singer of U2, to photo opportunities with Fidel Castro, but the victims of clerical sexual abuse are not seen as good PR. John Paul II made numerous speeches castigating 'particular offensive forms of injustice'. He singled out 'violence against women and against children of both sexes . . . forced prostitution and child pornography, and the exploitation of children in the workplace in conditions of veritable slavery'. But he never referred to the exploitation of children and their veritable sex slavery by thousands of his priests. Though many of the victims tried to meet him, there is not a single known instance of such a meeting.

The Pope's silence was deliberate. He brought with him from Poland to the Vatican practices that he had embraced throughout his life as a priest. They included an intense pathological hatred of any revelation that indicated the Catholic Church was not a perfect institution. All dissent must be kept behind closed doors, whether of Church politics, scandalous behaviour or criminal activity.

During the Pope's third visit to Austria in June 1998, he gave an illustration of his belief that child abuse and other such matters should not be discussed publicly. The Pope had strained to protect his close friend Cardinal Hans Hermann Groer against the demands of hundreds of thousands of Austrians for his resignation following compelling evidence that the Cardinal had sexually abused young boys. The Pope dismissed the evidence even though it demonstrated that the Cardinal had been a persistent paedophile over many years. Far more important to the Pope was that Cardinal Groer shared his Marian obsession. Eventually he

and his advisors were forced to acknowledge that the
controversy would not abate and a month before his
1998 visit the Pope had sadly been forced to agree to the
nationwide demand for Groer to leave his post. As he
arrived in Austria he was looking for scapegoats. In a
private meeting with the Austrian bishops he castigated
them roundly for failing to suppress the public outrage,
which had culminated in a petition by over 500,000 Austrians demanding a wide range of reforms. He was particularly incensed at the open debate on clerical sexual
abuse: 'like every house that has special rooms that are
not open to guests, the Church also needs rooms for talks
that require privacy.'

The insistence on such secrecy when it came to the
washing of the Church's dirty linen was a lifelong obsession
of Wojtyla. As a bishop in Cracow no public dissension, no
exposure of the Church's faults was the eleventh commandment. In 1980, the locking of the Dutch bishops in a Vatican
room until they repudiated the positions they had held since
Vatican Council II indicates how rigidly the late Pope
applied such tactics. To the Austrian bishops, Wojtyla made
it very clear that Cardinal Groer's crimes of repeated sexual
abuse of the young were as nothing compared to the crime
of publicising that abuse.

Three years later the papal preoccupation with secrecy
and cover-up was again demonstrated in a letter sent to
every bishop in the world. It came from Cardinal Joseph
Ratzinger in his capacity as head of the Congregation of the
Faith, but a subsequent apostolic letter from the Pope made
it clear that the 'initiative' was his. Ratzinger advised the
bishops of a new set of norms covering juridical control of
cases of sexual abuse by priests. The rules, which gave
control of any proceedings to Ratzinger's Congregation,
imposed 'pontifical secret' on all such cases, which would
be heard by an all-clerical jury. Priests judging the word of a

victim against the word of a fellow priest was not a scenario to inspire confidence. A Vatican-based bishop observed somewhat ruefully,

> 'these rules are going to give the appearance of a "cover-up". That's because they are a cover-up. As for what some are saying in this place that the secrecy is necessary to protect both the accuser and the accused – they have clearly to catch on to what in here would be a truly radical idea. That justice should not only be done. It should be seen to be done.'

Among the many victims of sexual abuse who would wholeheartedly endorse that sentiment are nine of the survivors of at least thirty who have alleged in sworn depositions that they were continually sexually abused by one particular priest over three decades from the 1940s into the 1960s. The priest in question is Father Marcial Maciel Degollado, the founder and superior general of the Legionaries of Christ. The nine men, now in their late fifties and mid-sixties had, as young boys, all been founder members of the Legionaries.

Juan J. Vaca was recruited by the Reverend Maciel Degollado at the age of ten while living with his parents in Mexico. Maciel told them that he 'saw something special in Juan' and offered the boy the chance of a good education at a seminary he was creating. Flattered, the parents accepted and when two years later Maciel told them that he would like to take Juan along with a number of other boys 'to my seminary in northern Spain for special training with the order', Juan recalled that there were 'tears from my mother but like my father she saw this as a wonderful opportunity'.

As Vaca recalled:

'we were isolated from the outside world by Maciel, all contacts were controlled by him and my mail was censored. After a short while in Spain he began to sexually abuse me. The first time this happened, when he had finished, I went to leave his room and he asked me where I was going. "To confession. I want absolution for what just happened." He told me that he would give me absolution, which he did.'

It was the beginning of years of sexual abuse in which the victim continually felt guilt but the perpetrator never appeared to. Maciel had explained that he regularly suffered from stomach pains and pain in his genitals, which could only be relieved by frequent masturbation. 'Soon,' Juan recalled, 'I became aware that he was abusing many of the other twenty-three children who were my school-mates.' For Juan the abuse continued for almost ten years during which he experienced 'an intense ethical and spiritual confusion, fear, shame and anxiety. I endured countless days of severe stress, and nights of debilitating sleeplessness'.

It was twelve years before Juan was permitted to see his parents again. The handsome young boy of ten was now a very disturbed twenty-two-year-old. Subsequently, while in the Legionaries residence in Rome, Juan summoned up the courage to confront Maciel and denounce him, but the young man's attempt to exorcise the demon he was confronting ended in the older man turning the tables and, after humiliating Juan, exiling him back to northern Spain as punishment. He was to remain there for six years.

Assuming that he had broken Juan's spirit, Maciel persuaded him to enter the priesthood. Juan, now a priest, was made Vice-Rector and Spiritual Director of the seminary in northern Spain. Subsequently four adolescent students came to him to denounce the Rector for sexually abusing them. Juan recalls the irony of that situation. 'I knew that the Rector, like me, was one of Maciel's original victims when we were all pre-adolescents. We now had second-generation abuse.'

Juan advised Maciel what had occurred.

'He gave me instructions that all traces of the abuse should be covered up. The perpetrator was fired from his post and immediately transferred secretly to a mission in the Yucatan peninsula of Mexico. For my "good work" in covering up the mess, the founder rewarded me with the appointment of superior and president of the Legion of Christ in the United States. In 1976 after five years in that post, I resigned the post and confronted Maciel and denounced him and three months later in October 1976 I formally denounced Maciel to the Vatican, through the proper channels of my bishop, the Reverend John R. McGann, and the Vatican embassy in Washington.'

Juan has since made an impressive success of his life. When I interviewed him in late 2004, I was aware that he had been a Professor of Psychology and Sociology at the Manhattan Campus of Mercy College for the past five years. All of the other surviving victims have also achieved considerable success in their respective lives. With regard to the sexual abuses they suffered from the Reverend Marcial Maciel Degollado, they do not seek financial compensation. They first wrote to Pope John Paul II soon after his election in 1978 and again in 1989 simply seeking official recognition that they had been sexually abused by a man he held in the highest regard. Monsignor John A. Alesandro, a canon lawyer in the Rockville Centre diocese, has confirmed that in both instances the correspondence seeking an investigation into Maciel had been forwarded to the Pope.

Over the years there have been several investigations of Father Maciel by the Vatican. These included a two-year period between 1956 and 1958 when he was suspended from his duties as superior General of the Legion after allegations of drug taking, misuse of funds and 'other improprieties'. Close study of Father Maciel's life indicates that either he has led a charmed existence or he has some very powerful protectors.

For the very first of his numerous pastoral pilgrimages, Pope John Paul II went to Mexico. Although a largely Catholic country, because of its history during the first half of the twentieth century, Mexico was constitutionally anti-clerical. Officially the Church did not exist. The Mexican bishops, not the government, had invited the Pope to a country which did not have diplomatic relations with the Vatican. The family of President Lopez Portillo were all devout Catholics and Father Maciel was a confidant of the President's mother and particularly the sister who was the President's confidential secretary. As a result Portillo listened to them and overrode the objections from his government ministers. Nonetheless the Pope was invited not as a head of state but as a visitor needing a visa.

During his visit to Mexico, the Pope and his secretary Father Dziwisz expressed their gratitude to Father Maciel for his timely intervention. They were both deeply impressed by the man who had created the beginnings of his 'spiritual army' while still a mere theology student of twenty. Before being inspired to do this in 1941, he had already been expelled from two seminaries for what his official history describes as 'misunderstandings' and had suffered a two-year suspension from his duties while a range of accusations had been investigated. Although in 1979 the Pope had only recently received extremely detailed allegations of continual sexual abuse by Maciel from nine of his victims, it did not give him or his secretary pause for thought. Maciel was never far from their side during the remainder of the trip.

The Legionaries of Christ blossomed through the ensuing years. They shared many characteristics with Opus Dei, and still do. Both are highly secretive, impose a regime of unquestioning total obedience, recruit aggressively, are wealthy and, most important, both have had the ear of the Pope and the most powerful papal secretary for seventy years. When Opus Dei and the Legionaries of Christ wanted to establish ecclesiastical universities in Rome (on the basis that only they could teach true orthodox principles) they were opposed by every current ecclesiastical university and the Congregation of Education. Discreet conversations were held with Dziwisz and after an appropriate time a papal decree announced the formation of two new universities.

The complaints by the nine former members of the Legionaries of Christ in 1989 were given further impetus when a tenth complaint from the terminally ill Juan Amenabar was sent to the Vatican in 1995. Amenabar was a former priest in Maciel's order, and as he lay dying, he dictated a damning indictment of the Rector. He had been moved to do so by a statement by the Pope a few months before, describing Maciel as 'an efficacious guide to youth'. In 1998, encouraged by the papal nuncio in Mexico City, the survivors brought a case against Maciel under canon law. They had never sought compensation, or even apologies; they sought only accountability by the Church for Maciel's sexual misconduct. Three years later in December 2001 the Vatican halted the canon law investigation, 'for the time being', without giving reasons or details.

In December 2004 the victims were told that a Vatican prosecutor from the Congregation of the Doctrine of Faith would be holding a formal inquiry. Juan J. Vaca remains sceptical. 'I have absolutely no confidence in the bureaucracy of the Vatican. Even now they are trying to cover up the fact that the Pope is dying.' Juan Vaca's misgivings were well founded. Cardinal Ratzinger secretly ordered the inquiry to stop 'to spare the Holy Father any embarrassment'.

The Vatican had less control over events in the United States. When Cardinal Law returned from the April 2002 meeting in the Vatican he tried to pick up exactly where he had left off. The Church resumed its delaying tactics to prevent courts and victims' lawyers getting access to files. As a result, the cardinal was ordered by judges to depose evidence in the case of Father Shanley in the ongoing cases against the defrocked John Geoghan. The spectacle was humiliating not merely for the cardinal but for every Roman Catholic in the United States. It would have been avoidable if Cardinal Law and his advisors had accepted that in a democracy no one is above the judicial process.

Father Shanley was charged with sexually abusing a six-year-old boy and continually raping him over many years. In February 2005 he was found guilty as charged and was sentenced to serve a term of twelve to fifteen years' imprisonment. The files showed that as late as 1997 Cardinal Law was still judging Shanley worthy of a warm glowing letter of introduction. It was as if the 1,600 pages in Shanley's file in the Boston chancery had never existed. Law claimed that he had transferred Shanley around the archdiocese 'without referring to the files'.

In September the initial claim by eighty-six victims of John Geoghan was settled at the reduced figure of $10 million. This left the way clear for the next claim by additional victims of the same former priest, whose number had risen to over 200.

While similar scenarios were being played out across the country, the bishops had also been addressing the task that they had brought back from the April meeting with the Pope. A month after they had departed from the Vatican in

May 2002, the Pope was obliged yet again to address the sex-abuse scandal – this time in private conversation with President George Bush. Confronted with the sight of large parts of the United States in tumult, the President (a born-again Christian) was anxious that his wide-ranging faith-based initiatives should not be damaged by the fall-out. The Pope assured him that Catholics in the US would overcome the current scandal and 'continue to play an important role in building American society'. This was of course the same American society that the Pope had declared was largely responsible for the crisis.

Wojtyla continued to avoid any close-up contact with the scandal and in July 2002 embarked on a twelve-day trip to Canada, Mexico and Guatemala. His failure to make even a symbolic stopover in the United States was seen by many American Catholics as a deliberate snub and yet further evidence of how much he was out of touch. Within the Vatican that reaction was seen as further evidence that the American response to the scandal was 'exaggerated, even hysterical'.

When Canadian victims of clerical sexual abuse re-quested a meeting with the Pope during the World Youth Day celebrations in Toronto they got a response similar to that given to the late Father Tom Economus: 'the Pope is far too busy to give time to such a meeting'. He was also too busy to address the subject of clergy sexual abuse at any point of his tour.

At much the same time the American bishops gathered in Dallas to find the solution to the problem. The buzzwords of the day were 'zero tolerance, one strike and you're out'. During the two-day conference Bishop Wilton Gregory made the most clear-cut statement of contrition by any senior figure of the Church since the crisis had begun. At the end of the conference he declared, 'From this day forward no one known to have sexually abused a child will work in the Catholic Church in the United States.' Nonetheless, the meeting struggled to define sexual abuse, and it struggled to provide safeguards for priests who might be unjustly accused. They failed to give a guarantee that the norms they were seeking to establish would be applied fairly. They neglected to affirm that the bishops themselves would be subject to the proposed discipline. Above all other omissions, one in particular was startling: they failed to address the root causes of clerical sexual abuse.

The lines of communication between Dallas and the Vatican began to get seriously busy. The Vatican was 'concerned that some of the proposals may well conflict with canon law'. The Vatican believed 'that some of your number are being unduly pressurised by both pressure groups (victim support groups) and the media'. The Vatican chose to ignore a current opinion poll that showed 87 per cent of US Catholics in favour of a zero-tolerance policy.

The Dallas document did not in fact call for an automatic defrocking or a total ban on priestly activities. A priest found guilty would be banned from public ministry and working with parishioners, but not automatically defrocked. Depending on the particular circumstances the priest would have the chance to function 'in a controlled environment' such as a 'monastery'. Though publicly the bishops approved the document by 239 to 13 votes, many were unhappy with the rulings, which would be binding, while others felt the directives and the new policy did not go far enough.

While the US bishops had been holding their meeting, Cardinal Oscar Rodriguez Maradiaga of Honduras, considered by many to be a leading contender as a Third World successor to Pope John Paul II, went public with views that a majority within the Vatican endorsed – but usually only in private. For Cardinal Maradiaga the reason that the United

States was enraged about clerical sexual abuse was the gross exaggeration 'by the media', which were intent on 'persecuting the Church' because of its firm stand on abortion, euthanasia, contraception and the death penalty. As for Cardinal Law, he was being victimised as if he were 'a defendant in a show trial staged by Nero or Stalin'. The Cardinal declared that Ted Turner, the founder of CNN news network, was 'openly anti-Catholic. Not to mention newspapers like the *New York Times*, the *Washington Post* and the *Boston Globe* which were protagonists of what I define as persecution against the Church.' He was also at pains to tell the world what a fine man Cardinal Law was.

Cardinal Maradiaga made his remarks during an interview with the Italian magazine *Thirty Days*. No sooner had he left the building than his Mexican colleague Cardinal Norberto Rivera entered and virtually repeated Maradiaga's denunciation. A few months later, a third Central American Cardinal, Miguel Obando y Bravo from Managua, Nicaragua, granted the same magazine an interview (nothing orchestrated, of course) and said, 'Anyone who attacks Cardinal Law today must not recognise the strength of his involvement, the weight of his ministry and the coherence of his life.' He felt sure that the faithful Catholics of Boston would recognise the 'golden nugget' in Cardinal Law's personality, which 'continues to shine'. The remainder of his interview was largely confined to yet another vilification of the American media.

As early as May yet another Latin American Cardinal, Eugenio Araujo Sales of Brazil, had led the attack on the allegations, describing them as 'over-exposed – many are old accusations – they account for less than a half of 1 per cent of 46,000 priests'. Disturbingly, this princely defence of Cardinal Law met with full Vatican approval. It showed up the gulf between the hierarchy and the victims and the overwhelming majority of rank-and-file Roman Catholics.

This gulf was again exposed in September 2002 when lawyers representing 250 plaintiffs who were suing the Boston archdiocese released personnel records on five priests showing that several bishops had known about the abuse allegations against the five for years, but left them in positions where they could abuse more children. One of the five had only been removed in March 2002, eight years after he was accused of abuse.

In November yet another judge, Constance Sweeney, delivered a handwritten note to the Boston archdiocese ordering the release of further thousands of documents covering the personnel files of priests accused of sexual misconduct. She complained bitterly that the archdiocese had engaged in a pattern of conduct designed to stall the implementation of prior court decisions. 'The court simply will not be toyed with,' she wrote.

In a separate order the judge strongly suggested that officials of the Boston archdiocese had conveyed an inaccurate picture of Church policies during their testimony on various sex-abuse cases. 'The available records raise significant questions of whether the archdiocese was really exercising the care they claimed to use in assigning offending priests.' She referred the case of Father Bernard Lane to the Attorney General of Massachusetts for possible perjury charges. What was unfolding in the Boston archdiocese had its counterpart in many another archdiocese and many another country.

While the events in Boston continued to move to an inevitable climax, the issue of establishing a national policy in the United States Church to respond to clerical sex abuse was back with the US bishops. The Vatican response to the Dallas proposal was to reject it. The Pope's zero-tolerance agenda of April 2002 was no longer his position in September. Though the US bishops had baulked at throwing sex abusers out of the priesthood, they had gone too far for the Pope and Ratzinger and their Vatican advisors, who favoured the opinions of the four Latin American Cardinals.

In the Pope's view, the Dallas accord could not be reconciled with the canon law, the rules that governed the Catholic Church. The Pope and his Heads of Congregations were primarily concerned with protecting the rights of the accused priest, and they were also unhappy with the American definition of sexual abuse. A fudge was in the making, which is best described as 'one strike and after every conceivable avenue of defence has been offered to you, if found guilty, you might be defrocked or you might be forced to wear civilian clothes and be confined to barracks'. Nowhere were the needs of the victim addressed or even recognised. Nowhere was there any mention of the legal necessity to inform civil authorities.

By early December 2002 the Pope's refusal to accept Cardinal Law's resignation in April had ensured months of constant humiliation for the Cardinal and continuous assault on the faith of over two million Catholics in Boston. During the first week of December the public release of yet more documents showed that the cover-up through the secret system had been even more extensive than previously realised. Confronted with lawsuits that could run into further compensation payouts of $100 million, the Cardinal obtained permission for his finance council to file for bankruptcy protection.

Boston priests soon began organising petitions calling for the resignation of Law. Many hundreds of angry Catholics gathered outside Boston's Holy Cross Cathedral to confront him. When they were told he had gone to Rome, they continued with their demonstration, demanding his removal. Three days later a furious Massachusetts Attorney General complained that the Boston archdiocese is 'using every tool and manoeuvre' to 'obstruct' an inquiry into sexual abuse by 'clergy'. Thomas Reilly told the *Boston Globe* that the archdiocese has been engaged in 'an elaborate and decades-long effort to cover up clerical misbehaviour'. On Friday 13 December the Boston Cardinal met with his protector and again offered his resignation. This time the Pope accepted it.

Bishop Richard Lennon was appointed apostolic administrator while the Vatican considered its options. Lennon announced that he hoped the archdiocese could avoid filing for bankruptcy. In the event they did but the price was high. Nine days after Cardinal Law's successor Archbishop Sean Patrick O'Malley was installed, at the beginning of August 2003, the archdiocese offered $55 million to settle some 500 outstanding clergy sex abuse lawsuits. The settlement would resolve claims from many hundreds of victims who had been abused as children by some 140 clergy within the Boston archdiocese. The offer was rejected.

While both sides considered their options, news broke that the former priest John Geoghan had been murdered in prison. A man who had caused so much pain, damage and heartache and destroyed countless lives had experienced prison's version of zero tolerance. A number of the plaintiffs who had just rejected the $55 million were men who had identified Geoghan as their abuser. Some of them began to feel the heat as legal advisors urged them to reconsider the rejected settlement. Some were in desperate need of a settlement, any settlement. In the event several busloads of lawyers sat down with Archbishop O'Malley and a new improved offer of $85 million was put on the table which was picked up.

When previous payments are included, the minimum figure paid out as compensation to the victims of clerical sexual abuse in the Boston archdiocese over a ten-year period is $116 million. The archdiocese was forced to put up its cathedral and seminary as collateral against loans it was forced to take out. Archbishop O'Malley has also decided to sell the Archbishop's residence and other church property worth many millions to help fund the compensation payout.

Archbishop O'Malley and men like him are clearly determined upon a new approach, which fully and honestly recognises the Catholic Church's culpability in this still-continuing scandal. At the present time such men are unfortunately in a minority within the higher reaches of the Church. Far too many still cling to a bizarre range of explanations either for the abuse or the Church's long-standing response.

The Latin American cardinals who saw a media conspiracy were not alone. US cardinals were largely at one with their brothers south of the border. Cardinal Theodore E. McCarrick of Washington spoke for many when he told the *Washington Post*, 'Elements in our society who are very opposed to the Church's stand on life, the Church's stand on family and the Church's stand on education . . . see this as an opportunity to destroy the credibility of the Church. And they are really working on it – and somewhat successfully.' Of course the *Washington Post* was regularly accused of being one of the leading media conspirators.

Others within the Roman Catholic hierarchy adopted a different line of attack. The Prefect of the Vatican's Congregation for the Clergy, Cardinal Dario Castrillón Hoyos, insisted that the problem of abusive priests was 'statistically minor . . . less than 0.3 per cent of priests are paedophiles'. Other clerics took a similar view without necessarily quoting the extraordinary figure of 0.3 per cent, plucked from the Roman or the Brazilian air. A document presented to Australia's bishops in late 1999 saw sexual abuse by clergy as part of the product of 'an all-male atmosphere within the seminaries that reflected male values and did not deal adequately with sexuality in general or with feminine issues in particular. As long as the culture of the Church does not put men and women on a basis of true equality, then women and children will remain vulnerable to abuse.'

Archbishop Rembert G. Weakland had an alternative explanation. 'Sometimes not all adolescent victims are so "innocent"; some can be sexually very active and aggressive and often quite streetwise.' The Archbishop, evidently speaking from personal experience, was subsequently forced to resign when it was revealed that he had paid a male lover nearly $500,000 to buy his silence. The money had allegedly come from diocesan funds.

Others blamed not streetwise adolescents but trial lawyers greedy for the Church's money. Maurice Healy, Director of Communications for the archdiocese of San Francisco, told the *New York Times* in early December 2002, 'There is a gold rush to get into the priest litigation business.' The next edition of the archdiocesan newspaper mailed to Catholics through Northern California headlined one article: 'Lawyers Aggressively Seek Sex Abuse Business', without mention of the initial aggression perpetrated on successive generations of young children. Healy's claim of a Church with 'limited resources' was made at precisely the same time that the new cathedral was opened in the south of California. Our Lady of Angels had been built at a cost of $200 million. At the time of the opening ceremony the Los Angeles diocese had seventy-two current or former priests under criminal investigation and was assailed with a large number of claims by victims of clerical abuse. Two weeks after the opening ceremonies, the archdiocese announced a deficit of $4.3 million and a range of cuts and closures in its counselling services.

Other reasons for the cause of the scandal put forward by elements of the Roman Catholic Church included:

'Paedophilia is spread by Satan . . . Catholic-bashing is fashionable. In fact the Protestants and the Baptists have even more paedophiles . . . the cover-ups were more out of frustration and igno-rance . . . the seminaries were infiltrated thirty to forty years ago by homosexuals and dissidents . . . Pope John XXIII and his Vatican Council are solely responsible.'

Those who blamed the Second Council managed to con-demn its rulings openly but simultaneously cited 'dissent' as the greatest reason for the sex abuse scandals. They meant dissent on issues of sexual morality that covered birth control, celibacy, homosexuality, abortion and divorce. Those who had identified widespread dissent from the Church's teaching on these subjects blamed not society in general but the bishops, whom they accused of failing to define doctrine firmly or to impose it, and declining to investigate credible evidence of violations. In early 2003 while priests as far apart as Pennsylvania and Hong Kong were pleading guilty to sexually abusing young boys, Bishop John McCormack of Manchester, New Hampshire, was attempting to justify his failure to inform the auth-orities of sexual abuse by priests. His deposition revealed that in the 1980s while working as an assistant to Cardinal Law he suppressed evidence concerning the sexual activities of a number of priests in Boston because he 'was acting as a priest and not as a social worker'. As the information had not come to him in a confessional setting, he was, in fact, obliged to pass it to the authorities. Bishop McCormack had also avoided asking the paedophile priests 'direct questions or making written notes'. He was aware that his records would be 'discoverable' if a victim filed suit against the archdiocese.

In March 2003 the Attorney General's office in New Hampshire issued a 154-page report accompanied by over 9,000 pages of documents which the Attorney General described as establishing that the Church leaders of the diocese of Manchester had been 'wilfully blind in dealing with clergy sex abuse and the related danger to children'.

In mid-2003 powerful independent evidence emerged that confirmed that at least part of the cause pointed to the bishops. One of the most positive initiatives to emerge from the Dallas conference of mid-2002 had been the creation of a lay panel whose brief was to investigate the sex abuse scandal. This national review board had the full power to question any cleric in the United States. The man appointed to chair the panel was former Oklahoma Governor Frank Keating. It was a highly popular appointment. Keating, a devout Catholic and a man of integrity, was viewed as honest and independent. Many of the bishops he interviewed gave the panel full cooperation; others did not. Keating compared the recalcitrants with Mafia leaders who pleaded the Fifth Amendment and refused to answer questions.

One of those who refused to cooperate was Cardinal Roger Mahony of Los Angeles. His personal skeletons dated back a long way and included a continuation of the cover-up of the seven priests who had repeatedly sexually abused Rita Milla. In 2001 it had been revealed that Cardinal Mahony had written to President Clinton during his second term requesting that the fifteen-year prison sentence passed on Los Angeles cocaine dealer Carlos Vignali be commuted. Clinton controversially obliged on his last day in office.

In late May 2002, just a few months before the national review board headed by Keating was created, a lawsuit was filed against Cardinal Mahony. Brought under the American federal racketeering laws designed to counter organised crime, the lawsuit was filed on behalf of four men who declared that they had been sexually molested as boys by Father Michael Baker. The men accused Mahony of conspiring to commit fraud and obstruct justice by covering up the activities of Baker. The plaintiffs also alleged that the cardinal paid off two of the victims in a $1.3 million settlement that required them to remain silent about the sexual abuse. A week before the lawsuit had been served, the Cardinal had admitted keeping secret for fourteen years a case of child abuse by Father Baker. Confronted by the lawsuit, Mahony dismissed the various allegations as 'groundless' but a short while later, when Frank Keating and his national review board came into town, Mahony was hostile.

The cardinal objected to being compared with the Mafia and forced Keating's resignation, thus confirming to many that some bishops were simply refusing to be accountable for their actions. Frank Keating's letter of resignation acknowledged what had been achieved during the year, including the appointment of a law enforcement professional to underline the message: 'Sex abuse is not just a moral lapse. It is a crime that should be fully prosecuted.' It continued:

'As I have recently said, and have repeated on several occasions, our Church is a faith institution. A home to Christ's people. It is not a criminal enterprise. It does not condone and cover up criminal activity. It does not follow a code of silence. My remarks, which some bishops found offensive, were deadly accurate. I make no apology. To resist grand jury subpoenas, to suppress the names of offending clerics, to deny, to obfuscate, to explain away, this is the model of a

criminal organisation, not my Church. The humiliation, the horrors of the sex scandal, must be a
poisonous aberration, a black page in our history that
cannot ever recur. It has been disastrous to the Church
in America.'

And not only to the American Church. The global reach of
the scandal was revealed by a report from Sister Maura
O'Donohue. Many believed that it inspired the unusually
explicit reference to sexual abuse in the Pope's address to
the Church of Oceania in 1998. Sister Maura's report was
submitted confidentially to Cardinal Eduardo Martinez,
prefect of the Vatican Congregation for Religious Life, in
February 1994. Sister Maura, a physician in the Order of
Medical Missionaries of Mary, had over forty years of
pastoral and medical experience. Her report was headed
'Urgent Concerns for the Church in the Context of HIV/
AIDS'.

Her investigations established that priests and religious were dying from AIDS-related illnesses. In many
of the countries where Sister Maura worked, prostitution was widely accepted. However, with the increased
awareness that prostitutes formed a high-risk group,
many men looked for an alternative. One group considered 'safe' targets for sexual activity were religious
sisters. Sisters began to report sexual abuse from their
professors and their teachers and sexual harassment
from men within the general population. The other
group that targeted women within religious orders were
priests. In one country, a Superior of a community of
sisters was approached by priests requesting that sisters
be made available for sexual favours. When the Superior
refused, the priests explained that if she did not
cooperate they would be obliged to 'go to the village
and find women and risk getting AIDS'.

Sister Maura's report irrefutably established a shocking catalogue of sexual abuse. She observed,

'It does not apply to any single country or even continent, nor indeed to any one group or all members of society. In fact the following examples derive from experience over a six-year period and relate to incidents in some twenty-three countries in five continents: Botswana, Brazil, Colombia, Ghana, India, Ireland, Italy, Kenya, Lesotho, Malawi, Nigeria, Papua New Guinea, Philippines, South Africa, Sierra Leone, Uganda, Tanzania, Tonga, United States of America, Zambia, Zaire, Zimbabwe.'

It was her devout hope that the report would 'motivate appropriate action especially on the part of those in positions of Church leadership and those responsible for formation'. The report detailed priests and bishops abusing and exploiting their powers to indulge in sexual relations. Potential candidates to religious life were coerced into granting sexual favours to ensure they obtained the required certificates and/or recommendations. Sisters who became pregnant were forced to leave their congregation, but the priests responsible continued in their ministry.

The report also contained many positive recommendations to overcome the abuse of women within the Church. A year after she submitted the report to Cardinal Martinez, no one in the Vatican had taken any action other than to invite Sister Maura and her colleagues to a meeting with Martinez and three members of his staff. As she dryly observed in a subsequent memorandum, 'It was clear that there was no prearranged agenda.'

Subsequently other concerned senior women from religious orders created similar reports. Still there was no action either from Cardinal Martinez or any other senior

Vatican figure. The Pope's brief comments quoted earlier had still not been made public when in great frustration some of the authors of the reports contacted the *National Catholic Reporter* in early 2001. As a result, the newspaper ran a cover story on 16 March 2001. *La Repubblica*, Italy's largest daily, followed up four days later with a long report on the issue.

The Vatican was forced to respond. Its statement came not from the Pope or Cardinal Martinez but from the ubiquitous Navarro-Valls. 'The problem is known, and is restricted to a geographically limited area.' That comment should be compared with the list of countries given earlier, a list that is by no means complete. The statement continued,

> 'The Holy See is dealing with the question in collaboration with the bishops, with the Union of Superiors General (USG) and with the International Union of Superiors General (USIG). The work has two sides, the formation of persons and the solution of single cases.'

Setting up committees does not constitute a solution. No positive action had been taken by the Holy See over the seven years since they had first been made fully aware of this additional dimension of sexual abuse by Sister Maura O'Donohue and other experts. Far from seeking a 'solution of single cases', the Holy See needed a root and branch purge within the ranks of the clergy. The Vatican spokesman concluded, 'Certain negative situations cannot cause to be forgotten the frequently heroic fidelity of the great majority of male religious, female religious and male priests.'

Navarro-Valls' claim for the 'heroic fidelity of the great majority' flies in the face of powerful research evidence. Researchers at the Saint Louis University carried out a national survey in the United States. It was completed in 1996 but intentionally never publicised. It estimated that a minimum of 34,000 Catholic nuns, about 40 per cent of all nuns within the United States, had suffered some form of sexual trauma.

Largely financed by a number of Catholic religious orders, the researchers dealt with three areas of sexual victimisation: childhood sexual abuse where the victim is younger than eighteen years, sexual exploitation/coercion by those in a position of power over the nun and, thirdly, sexual harassment at work and within the community of sisters. At the time of the survey there were approximately 89,000 Catholic sisters in the United States and about 85,000 (95 per cent) were members of active religious institutes or communities. The fifteen-page survey was sent to 2,500 names randomly selected from the 25,000 made available to the University team. Every American state was represented plus additional names working in a number of foreign countries.

The responses showed that 18.6 per cent had been sexually abused as children. Most of the abusers were male with brothers, uncles, male strangers, male family friends, fathers and male cousins topping the list in that order. Clergymen and nuns accounted for nearly 10 per cent of the child abusers. In the second stage 12.5 per cent had been sexually exploited and in the third stage 9.3 per cent had been sexually harassed during their work as a religious. The results also suggested that taking their entire life from childhood to the present time 40 per cent had suffered some form of sexual trauma and nearly 22 per cent had been abused during their religious life. As the research team observed, 'The interpretations and implications of these events for the individual woman and religious life in general are compelling.'

Catholic priests and nuns formed the largest group of

abusers of women religious, frequently when acting as a spiritual advisor to the victim. Other roles that were identified for the sexually abusing priests included pastor, retreat director, counsellor and mentor. The most frequent roles for nuns guilty of sexual abuse were mentor, formation director, religious superior and teacher.

In July 2001, representatives of 146 religious, women's rights and human rights groups launched an international campaign aimed at pressurising the Vatican to end the Catholic clergy's sexual abuse and sexual violence against nuns and lay women. Earlier the same year the European Parliament passed an emergency motion censuring the Vatican and requesting 'that the Vatican seriously examine every indication of sexual abuse committed in the heart of its organisation'. It also demanded that the Vatican 're-establish women in their posts in the religious hierarchy, who were removed from their responsibilities because they called the attention of their superiors to these abuses'. The Holy See was also asked to cooperate with any judicial enquiry. As of early 2005 it had yet to respond.

While the petitioners to the Vatican waited, clerical sexual abuse continued to be exposed. In May 2004 Margaret Kennedy, a Catholic who founded Christian Survivors of Sexual Abuse, revealed to me some of the details of a study yet to be published. She had previously compiled details of 120 cases of alleged sexual abuse of women by clergy but her latest report deals with a further sixty cases. Just as sexual abuse of children and adults is not confined to Roman Catholic clerics, the same applies to the sexual abuse of women. All faiths have ministers who are sexual predators. Among the new sixty cases were twenty-five that involved clerics from the Church of England, twenty-five from the Roman Catholic Church and the remainder spread among Methodists, Baptists and Presbyterians.

The report noted:

'Approximately 50 per cent of the clergy involved in these particular cases are married men, which rather demolishes the proposition that celibacy is at the heart of the problem of clerical sexual abuse. It's not about celibacy, it is about abuse of power.'

Margaret Kennedy believes that most of the clergy involved should be treated as sex offenders:

'The priest in his capacity as a professional must accept that when a woman comes to him seeking help, spiritual direction, counselling and advice that there are boundaries. The woman is a client and should be regarded at all times as such. We are not talking about a social meeting on a golf course. I actually believe that the client should be able to walk into a meeting with her priest stark naked and that the priest should still be able to hold a boundary between himself and his client.' Many of Margaret Kennedy's case studies dealt with the priest or the minister within a pastoral relationship moving inexorably to sexual abuse. 'The same rules that apply to doctors, physiotherapists and psychologists should apply to clergy.'

The testimony against the men included in Kennedy's report had a very familiar ring: 'He would tell me this was our secret and I shouldn't say anything to anyone. This was what God wanted – God would be pleased with me.' Or, 'He told me it was God's will to have sex with me and when I turned him down that I wasn't being obedient to God . . . He started off trying to kiss me and fondle my breasts.' Father Tamayo and his fellow priests were saying exactly the same things to Rita Milla during the 1970s. Father

Gauthe repeatedly told his altar boys that what he was doing to them was God's will. Virtually every clerical sexual abuser that has been exposed over the years has brought God into the equation and created a blasphemous and sacrilegious ménage à trois.

The exact nature of the coercion varies from abuser to abuser. Father Kamal Bathish did not invoke the Almighty directly but used a very effective technique of making his victim dependent on himself as her spiritual mentor. In 1983 Pauline Cunningham had just finished a three-year commission as a nurse in the British Army when she saw an advertisement for volunteer nurses in Jerusalem. At the time she had been considering a future in nursing in California. 'Working there as a nurse, meeting a great American, getting married, having three children, that was my dream.' Instead she found herself working in St Joseph's, a small Christian hospital in East Jerusalem, where her childhood Catholic faith was reawakened. She began to attend Mass again: 'Well, something just touched me. I'd always worked as a nurse and worked towards physically helping people to heal but frequently thought there was something missing.'

In April 1985 she entered a Carmelite Convent in Bethlehem as a novitiate. Pauline assumed that within a Carmelite Order all was peace, harmony and tranquillity but she was very rapidly disabused. Nothing had prepared her for the bitchiness, the warring factions and the frequent disappearance of Christianity:

'The legitimate Superior was rather weak. The sister who had previously been Prioress for a long time was very into power games . . . I was totally shocked. I have been brought up very strictly in the Catholic faith and never for one moment had I thought that nuns and priests could bitch and gossip, be so uncharitable and behave as if they were living in a secular world rather than a Carmelite Order.'

Pauline, or Sister Marie Paul as she had become, and another novitiate complained to the Latin Patriarch's office who had overall responsibility and authority over the Order:

'They came and saw us a couple of times but their response was, "Just accept the suffering. This is Jerusalem. You will have to accept the unfairness and all that occurs within the Order. It is part of your particular suffering towards your personal purification."'
This advice had come from the Patriarch's secretary, Father Kamal Bathish.

Pauline attempted to follow the advice but by September 1986 the Mother Superior was constantly seeking *her* guidance and support; the novitiate was completely out of her depth and decided to leave the convent. Two years later in 1988, still seeking a form of life with a religious base, she returned to Jerusalem. Out of courtesy she advised the Patriarch's office of her return. At this time she discussed her future with Father Bathish and her plans to resume nursing. Bathish urged her to become a 'consecrated person', an individual who while living and working in the secular world offers his or her life in the service of the Church. In essence it was a lay vocation, with a life of poverty, chastity and obedience. Such a commitment appealed to Pauline who saw it as 'an appropriate way of being of service'. Bathish suggested a fellow priest, Father Grech, as her spiritual director. The kindly and thoughtful Bathish also said he would 'always be available for any future problems you might have'.
Pauline recalls that Bathish became 'a good listener,

particularly after I had made a complaint to him concerning another priest who had attempted to sexually assault me.' The incident had occurred just a month after her return in March 1988. It left Pauline even more dependent on Father Bathish for support and counselling. The secret system was applied to Father Peter Madros, the priest who had allegedly assaulted Pauline, and he was moved to another location, Biet Sahour. Soon the Patriarch's office received another complaint after Madros had harassed a married woman. Yet again he was quietly moved.

Pauline found it difficult to relate to Father Grech. He would never discuss the events that had occurred at the Convent, events that Pauline was still attempting to come to terms with. Bathish was different and by early August 1988 the thirty-one-year-old nurse and the forty-six-year-old priest had established a mutually trusting relationship. She turned to him increasingly for support and guidance:

'Then one evening, he kissed me. I was totally and utterly astonished. Oh my God! I just didn't say anything. You know when you are out with someone and they suddenly kiss you. You don't push them away or make a scene or say anything. You just go really quiet and back away so that you don't embarrass the other person. I thought, well I'm not going to say anything, maybe it was just a one-off. I valued his support and his understanding of my situation and of the background I had come from and I valued that far far more. So I just kept on seeing him and talking to him. But the more I saw him the more insistent he became sexually. Sometimes when I cried, he would kiss me or touch me and become more comforting. I had a very strong spiritual dependence on him. Not physical, not at all, but I did whatever he told me to do. I had misgivings, I felt guilt, I felt shame.'

Over the ensuing nine months this curious relationship continued to develop, with Pauline deriving spiritual comfort and Father Bathish obtaining physical satisfaction. The kissing became fondling, and then the priest persuaded her to relieve his frustration by masturbating him, then oral sex. Father Bathish belongs to the same sexual school of ethics as former President Bill Clinton: anything short of sexual penetration was not sexual intercourse, not even for a priest who has taken a vow of chastity. Pauline continued to display an almost reverential attitude to Father Bathish:

> 'He used to fondle me and put his hands up my skirt, things like that and I used to push his hands away but I never actually verbally said the word "no" because I thought that to do that would embarrass him or humiliate him and I had no wish to do either ... I thought that if I did that he would be angry and then I'd lose that support, the moral support, the comfort – not so much the comfort but the understanding and care that he gave me that I needed at the time very much.'

I questioned her closely about the obvious paradox of suffering humiliation rather than the risk of causing it, of showing such consideration for his feelings while he demonstrably had shown none for hers. During her time in the convent she had strenuously objected to behaviour from others that was mild in comparison to this priest's behaviour. While a novitiate she had taken strong exception to any invasion of her privacy yet here she was accepting a much more profound invasion. Why accept such behaviour? She replied, 'Because it was somebody that I knew could understand me and understand where I was coming from, somebody that you could share things with. That you could trust.'

A year later in July 1989 Pauline was offered the opportunity of running a guest house that was owned by the Patriarchate, the Knight's Palace. She had made a number of attempts to end the sexual element of her relationship with Father Bathish while rather unrealistically maintaining the spiritual aspect. Now she tried again but without success. The priest still represented someone to turn to when there was a problem. By the summer of 1992 their relationship was an open secret within the religious community. There was no question in the minds of the various priests when it came to apportioning blame. The fault was Pauline's and hers alone. The injustice was compounded when Pauline was dismissed. From that date Pauline Cunningham, the woman who went to Jerusalem seeking a religious life, began fighting for justice. Both elements were to prove elusive.

Eventually, after a criminal trial that started in March 1997 alleging sexual exploitation and 'constructive rape', the patriarchate of Jerusalem was found guilty and Pauline was awarded 240,000 shekels, about £25,000. The trial ended in 2003. Subsequently she was also awarded 5,000 shekels after the Jerusalem hierarchy had tried to prevent publication of the initial ruling.

Father Tom Doyle is familiar with the case, and has sworn an affidavit in support of Pauline's struggle to establish the truth. For him, this is

'a classic case of reverential fear. This fear is induced in a person by reason of the force of the other person's stature, position, rank or special relationship with the victim . . . The victim has such an emotional and psychological respect for or fear for the one imposing the force that he or she cannot act in any other way than the way the person wishes. In Catholic culture it is common for lay people, children, or others to be induced by this force when in the presence of clerics.

Catholics are indoctrinated from their childhood that priests take the place of Jesus Christ and are to be obeyed at all costs and never questioned or criticised. This exalted position is even more firmly rooted in a Catholic's mind and emotions if the person is a high-ranking cleric or holds an exalted title such as "monsignor" or is a bishop.'

During Pauline's relationship with Father Bathish, he became first a monsignor and then a bishop. Father Doyle observed,

'The trauma bond that comes into existence in a cleric–lay relationship, especially a sexual relationship, is a pathological or sick bond that becomes firmer and sicker the longer the relationship goes on. A common example of such a bond is that which exists between a battered spouse and her battering husband as she continues to go back to him in spite of the violence.'

The Latin Patriarch, Michel Sabbah, consistently refused over many years to meet Pauline Cunningham, despite the fact that there were at least four other women who had suffered sexual abuse from Bishop Bathish, and that the bishop has admitted the truth of Pauline's allegations. He made this confession to a commission of inquiry set up by the Patriarch. The Patriarch is directly answerable to the Pope, yet the Vatican's position is that the case is a matter for the Patriarch.

The closed-doors Vatican seminar on clerical sexual abuse conducted in April 2003 had ended with the content of the discussions, the agenda and the conclusions all a closely guarded secret. It was a further ten months before the Vatican deigned to share a little of what had transpired.

Typically out of touch, the Vatican airily declared that the proceedings of the seminar 'might be available in late March or might remain a private document available only to bishops and to consulting professionals working with the bishops' approval'.

The seminar had heard from a dozen or so eminent doctors and psychiatrists. The experts were all of one mind: they were all apparently horrified that the Dallas meeting of US bishops should have advocated zero tolerance on abuse. At a brief press conference held at the Vatican in late February 2004, Bishop Elio Sgreccia, the President of the Pontifical Academy for Life, summed up the most disastrous conclusion reached during the previous year's Vatican seminar. He said that the specialists assembled by the Vatican had concluded

'It is possible and necessary to find an approach even for priests who are guilty of sexual abuse, to pursue treatment and rehabilitation and not to abandon them or consider them useless to the Church.'

During the seminar, a number of the experts including the American psychiatrist Martin Kafka spoke of the 'excessively punitive' policies adopted by the American hierarchy. Kafka and his colleagues were sure they knew the way forward. Their approach was based on professional self-delusion and threatened to subvert the course of justice. The most telling indictment of the conclusions of the seminar is in the selection criteria for those invited. Bishop Sgreccia explained that 'The institutions they represent are *de facto* used by bishops' conferences for the treatment of priests and religious.' It was akin to inviting the makers of the SS *Titanic* to build an icebreaker. Despite an almost unbroken record of failure in treating clerical sexual abusers, the chosen experts expressed themselves dogmatically. The

Canadian psychologist William Marshall told the Vatican officials that zero tolerance for sex abusers is

> 'a disaster. If I kick this fellow out of the Church and he loses his job, his income, his health benefits and all of his friends . . . with no other skills to get a job, that's not the conditions to ensure a former priest won't commit more abuse.' He claimed that a number of American bishops and clergy came up to him at the first break and said, 'That's exactly what the bishops in the US need to hear.'

Apart from turning bishops into welfare officers for clerical sex abusers, the approach of the seminar sought to keep abusers away from judicial investigation or trial. This is the ultimate irony: after turning themselves into secular priests, psychiatrists, psychologists and doctors set themselves up as judge and jury over priests who sin. From Pope John Paul II down to the most recently appointed bishop, in any aspect of the sexual abuse scandal, the first line of defence for the Church has been:

> 'We did not know. We did not understand. We relied on our own judgements when confronted with clerical sexual abuse. There were no data, no information, no studies. There was nothing available on this and associated behavioural problems.'

The falsity of that defence was demonstrated by Monsignor Charles Scicluna, an official of Cardinal Ratzinger's Congregation for the Doctrine of the Faith, during the secret Vatican seminar. The experts who had been invited were all non-Catholics and Monsignor Scicluna gave them a much needed history lesson on how the Church had dealt with clerical sex abusers in earlier times. He quoted among others Pope Alexander II, at the Third Lateran Council in 1179 on sexual abusers. 'If they are clerics, they will be dismissed from the clerical state or else will be confined to monasteries to do penance.' Scicluna also quoted Pope Pius V declaring in 1568 that sexual abusers 'must be handed over to the secular authorities for punishment and if he is a cleric will be demoted from everything'.

My informant gave no clue as to the response of Messrs Kafka and Marshall to the history lesson. For good measure Monsignor Scicluna also drew attention to the early twentieth-century Church position quoting from the 1917 Code of Canon Law: 'Priests who engage in sexual misconduct with children will be suspended, they will be declared unworthy, they will be deprived of any office, benefice, dignity, or responsibility they may have.' However, he does not appear to have quoted from the 1984 revised Code of Canon Law, whose language on the offence of sexual abuse of a minor (meaning under the age of sixteen) was much softer. It said that the abuser 'is to be punished with just penalties, not excluding dismissal from the clerical state if the case so warrants'. For much of its existence and until six years *after* Karol Wojtyla was elected Pope, the Church applied a policy of zero tolerance without exception or excuse. How did it manage to forget its history?

Having quoted copiously from the history of how the Roman Catholic Church had dealt with sexual abuse over the centuries Monsignor Scicluna unfortunately failed to examine the other side of the coin. What *contemporary* information was available to the Church's bishops and cardinals? In case after case, the cover-up, the lies, the deceit, the careful use of the 'secret system' gives the lie to the repeated suggestion that 'there was so little known at the time and the cardinal or the bishop were guilty only of ignorance'. If those who protected the sexually abusing priest genuinely believed, as they have claimed, that all could be cured by the power of prayer, then why go to such elaborate lengths to hide the crime? Why not have an open day of prayer for the offending priest at his local church? Is it possible to believe that the bishops and cardinals were unaware of the necessity of removing paedophiles from any possible contact with children?

As of the mid-1980s, the time of the Father Gauthe case, the Church had access to abundant studies of the origins and effects of clerical sexual abuse. One was *The Catholic Priest in the United States: Psychological Investigations* by Father Eugene C. Kennedy and Victor Heckler. This ground-breaking work paid particular attention to the emotional and developmental problems of priests. The authors concluded that 7 per cent of priests were emotionally developed, 18 per cent developing, 66 per cent underdeveloped and 8 per cent maldeveloped. The extraordinarily high percentages indicating emotional immaturity are illuminating. The personal profile of the immature reminds me vividly of the description of psychopaths by Sir David Henderson to the Royal Commission on Capital Punishment in the early 1950s:

'They are dangerous when frustrated. They are devoid of affection, are cold, heartless, callous, cynical and show a lack of judgement and forethought, which is almost beyond belief. They may be adult in years, but emotionally they remain as dangerous children whose conduct may revert to a primitive, sub-human level.'

Father Kennedy's study had been commissioned by the National Conference of Catholic Bishops in the late 1960s. It was delivered to them in 1971. It would have been an invaluable aid towards understanding the mind of the sexually abusing priest, particularly those priests who abused young children and adolescents. However, the bishops did not even discuss the questions raised within the report, let alone implement its suggestions. They simply ignored their own report.

The Church could also have consulted the centres for the care of 'problematic priests' run by the Servants of the Paraclete, the first of which was opened in Jemez Spring in New Mexico in 1949. It also included the records of the Seton Psychiatric Institute, a Catholic-owned and Catholic-operated hospital in Baltimore, Maryland, established in 1844. Richard Sipe worked at Seton from 1967 to 1970. He was professed a Benedictine monk in 1953 and ordained a Roman Catholic priest in 1959. He is also a qualified psychotherapist and psychiatrist. He recalled,

'Shortly after I was ordained in 1959 I was assigned as a teacher and counsellor in a parish high school. This was my first introduction to parish life and the secret world of sexual activity on the part of Catholic priests and religious with both minors and adults. I also became aware of the "secret system".'

It was this revelation that prompted Sipe's interest in counselling Catholic priests and religious. It was to become a life's work. He revealed to me that Seton had kept records all the way back to 1917, many of which include priestly sexual abuse cases:

'[Case of clerical sexual abuse] was frequently masked by fellow priests working in the clinic . . . deep depression, or "his activities have led to heavy drinking" but sexual abuse was the fundamental problem. By the time I came to work there in the late sixties virtually all referrals to Seton were for priests and religious for sexual contact involving minors. The referral was a device used by the Church to avoid public exposure or a court action.'

Sipe then continued to confine the extent of the problem and his response to such cases:

> 'I collaborated with colleagues from many countries who were working in the same field. The Netherlands, Ireland, England, Australia, India and Africa . . . Canada, Spain, much of the Third World. It's global.'

He also put paid to the lie that the bishops could not have known the extent of clerical abuse. Not only was data, the information, the records on clerical sexual abuse at the various other clinics and hospitals available to any bishop who wished to be informed on paedophilia, Sipe also stated that the bishops 'were fully acquainted anyway'.

There was certainly no reason for the Church to be shocked or ignorant about clerical sexual abuse when the Gauthe case erupted in 1985. Apart from the sources already mentioned, the Church could have read legal articles on clergy malpractice, or consulted reference books such as the *Diagnostic and Statistical Manual Of Mental Disorders* which defined paedophilia as follows:

A The act or fantasy of engaging in sexual activity with prepubertal children as a *repeatedly* preferred or exclusive method of achieving sexual excitement.

B If the individual is an adult, the prepubertal children are at least ten years younger than the individual. If the individual is a late adolescent, no precise age difference is required, and clinical

judgement must take into account the age difference as well as the sexual maturity of the child.

In the United Kingdom Bishop Murphy O'Connor could
have referred to *Child Abuse and Neglect: A study of
prevalence in Great Britain* or at least twelve other studies
that were all in print at the time he was ignoring advice and
protecting a paedophile. Better still, he could have contacted the Servants of the Paraclete in Gloucestershire, an
organisation with over thirty years' experience in the treatment of paedophiles – where he himself had sent the serial
paedophile Father Hill. Instead the wretched Hill was given
carte blanche by the man who sits today at the head of the
Roman Catholic Church in England.

The Vatican was fully aware of many of these studies. In
1971 for example, it invited Doctor Conrad Baars and Dr
Anna Terruwe to present their paper dealing with 'the causes,
treatment and prevention of emotional immaturity and ill-
ness in priests' to a meeting sponsored by the Synod of
Bishops. Among those listening in the audience was Cardinal
Wojtyla, who was elected to the Synod Council at the end of
that Synod. Dr Baars' report was based on the medical
records and files of 1,500 priests treated for mental problems.
A Dutch-born Catholic psychiatrist, Baars concluded that
less than 15 per cent of priests in Western Europe and North
America were emotionally fully developed. 20 to 25 per
cent had serious psychiatric difficulties that often resulted
in alcoholism and 60 to 70 per cent suffered from lesser
degrees of emotional immaturity. The report made ten
recommendations, including a more effective vetting of
potential priests. None were implemented.

While an overwhelming majority of Catholics polled
around the world continue to condemn the Church's
response to clerical sexual abuse, the Vatican maintains
its traditional long view of history. Although 80 per cent of

American Catholics polled by Zogby believe that the legal system and not the Church should process allegations, the Vatican listens only to its hand-picked experts, congregations and bishops who continue to believe in keeping the problem within the Church. In Dublin's recent Royal College of Surgeons survey, 75 per cent of those polled consider the Church's response to be 'inadequate', 50 per cent believe the damage done to the Church in Ireland to be 'irreparable' and 92 per cent do not think that a priest who has abused children should return to ministry. While the rank and file made abundantly clear what they believed should happen within their Church, the Vatican continued with the old way and ignored the congregation. Instead, it heeds the words of psychologists who wish to show the sex abuser every conceivable consideration.

On more than one occasion, Pope John Paul II declared that secular politicians must adjust civil law to God's. However, in regard to financial and sexual crime he practised a third way – protecting clergy who reject both the civil law and God's. Some of his defenders with no sense of irony berated reporters and journalists for what they call 'media abuse' yet they ignored the frequent acknowledgements of law enforcement officials who applauded the media's efforts to get to the truth. For example, District Attorney Martha Coakley of Massachusetts publicly thanked the press after the arrest of Father Paul Shanley. She acknowledged that her office had no resources for manhunts and thanked the media for tracking Shanley down. She also acknowledged the court's debt to the writers who devoted time, energy and money to researching and profiling the 'predator priests like Shanley'.

This is clearly another aspect of the scandal that has angered the Vatican. Not only are they opposed to the due legal process in spirit, they also object to it in practice. The Arizona District Attorney, Rick Romley, wrote to Vatican

Secretary of State Cardinal Angelo Sodano requesting that the Vatican instruct priests that had been indicted in Arizona in child abuse cases to return to the State. His letter came back unopened with a covering note: 'The item here enclosed is returned to sender because it has been refused by the rightful addressee.' Romley was pursuing a number of fugitive priests, including one hiding in Rome and others in Mexico and Ireland.

If the Catholic Church in Massachusetts has finally faced up to its responsibilities, in many another part of the United States the Church is fighting a bitter rearguard action reminiscent of Cardinal Law's years of lies, prevarication and deceit. In Rhode Island, for example, thirty-eight victims of sexual abuse have waited so long for their lawsuits to be resolved that four of the eleven accused priests have died. The Diocese of Providence has succeeded in delaying the legal process for more than ten years by every conceivable device.

In July 2003, to the undisguised glee of the reactionary element within the Church and certain insurance companies, the United States Supreme Court ruled by five to four as unconstitutional a California law removing the statute of limitation on past crimes, thus allowing prosecution for sexual abuse crimes. In a dissenting opinion, Justice Anthony Kennedy wrote: 'The court . . . disregards the interests of those victims of child abuse who have found the courage to face their accusers and bring them to justice.' Many bishops worldwide would like to see similar statutory limitations introduced. Off the record, they will admit that their view is heavily coloured by their financial advisors, their insurance companies and their lawyers. To avoid going into financial bankruptcy many a bishop is rapidly exhausting his moral capital.

In England and Wales, the Church shows a similar ingrained reluctance to face up to its legal responsibilities.

It continues to hide behind the curious argument that it is not responsible for its individual priests. It claims that as priests are 'office-holders', they are neither employed nor self-employed. The spokesman of the Catholic Primate of England and Wales attempted to justify the secrecy clauses in agreements made with the victims by claiming, 'These are not gagging orders; these are agreements drawn up by solicitors. The Church does not draw up these agreements.' Of course, the Church gives no instructions to its solicitors. It meekly signs agreements then hands over the compensation payments (which the Vatican has always condemned).

In late November 2003 Archbishop Daniel Pilarczyk of Cincinnati walked into court after a bitter eighteen-month battle during which the archdiocese had used every legal device possible to block prosecution access to its Church records on paedophile priests. He publicly admitted that on at least five separate occasions between 1979 and 1982 archdiocese officials were told of allegations concerning sexual abuse of children by priests and 'knowingly failed' to report them. It was an historic admission, the first time that an archdiocese had been convicted for its role in clerical sexual abuse cases.

Pilarczyk had been one of the bishops who had failed to act upon the recommendations within the 1985 report written by Father Doyle, Father Peterson and lawyer Ray Mouton. In 1992 Archbishop Pilarczyk in response to a letter from Tom Doyle revealed why the report had been ignored. 'The fact remains that your report presented no new issue (of which the NCCB was unaware) or information that required some materially different response.' Perhaps if the Archbishop had studied the report more closely he would not have found himself in court. Having accepted the guilty plea judge Richard Niehaus fined the archdiocese the nominal sum of $10,000. He then revealed that he was a Catholic as he looked directly at the Archbishop and continued, 'I believe that a religious organisation not only should follow the civil law but also the moral law.'

Two months later in January 2004, with the Church hierarchy in the United States and Rome deeply split over the correct response to clerical sexual abuse, yet another scandal began to unfold. The Archdiocese of Washington (DC) was informed by a law firm that it represented at least ten alleged victims of a sex abuse ring in a suburban Maryland parish. Between the 1960s and the 1980s 'dozens' of boys aged between eight and sixteen years had been treated as 'sexual servants' by a ring of priests based in the parish. By the end of 2003 the archdiocese had announced that twenty-six priests had 'been credibly accused of sex abuse over the past 56 years'. In January 2004 that total rose to over thirty.

In February 2004, a week after the Vatican had released a minimum of information on the evidence and conclusions of the closed-doors seminar of 2003, the American Bishops' National Review Board released a detailed report covering a year-long investigation into sexual abuse by clergy in the US Catholic Church. Many had hoped that this independent review would finally produce unassailable facts and figures. The Review Board had been greatly assisted by the John Jay College of Criminal Justice who had been commissioned by the Board to develop empirical data on the nature and scope of 'the problem that precipitated the crisis'.

Neither the Board nor the John Jay College were met with open doors in every diocese. They nonetheless created a report with much invaluable information, which reflects great credit on the Board and its Chairman, Governor Keating, and on the tenacious questioning of the John Jay team. According to the report, Church records indicate that between 1950 and 2002, 4,392 priests were accused of engaging in sexual abuse with a minor. This figure represented 4 per cent of the 109,694 priests in active ministry during that period. There were approximately 10,667 reported child victims of clergy sexual abuse during this time and the Church expended more than $500 million in dealing with the problem.

As the report notes, 'In very few cases, however, did the diocese or religious order report the allegation to the civil authorities.' As a consequence 'more than 100 priests or former priests served time in prison for conduct involving sexual abuse of a minor'. Put another way – less than 200 out of a total of 4,392 priests were imprisoned.

Victim survivor groups have denounced the report as 'a whitewash' and claim that the real figures for clerical sexual abusers during the period are far higher. The report's comment that 56 per cent of the accused priests had only one reported allegation levied against them provoked much criticism from experts. As Father Tom Doyle observed, 'This statement defies the data provided by mental health professionals concerning the average number of victims of sexual abusers, both paedophiles and ephebophiles (abusers of adolescents).' Tom Doyle speaks with a wealth of personal knowledge on the subject – mainly acquired since he was forced out of the Vatican diplomatic service by a faction within the American bishops. During the intervening twenty years Doyle has been involved in over 700 cases of clerical sexual abuse, either advising or testifying on behalf of the victims.

The figure of $500 million that is given for the cost of the scandal to date is widely seen as a serious underestimate. For example, it does not include the $85 million paid out by the Boston Archdiocese. The amount generally accepted is $1 billion. Even this can be comfortably absorbed by the US Catholic Church. Its annual revenue is in excess of $8 billion, and it owns real estate with an estimated value between $10 and $15 billion.

As many as 20 per cent of the allegations were not subjected to any investigation by the dioceses in question because 'the priest was deceased or inactive at the time of the allegation'. A further 10 per cent were characterised as 'unsubstantiated', which as the authors of the report note 'does not mean that the allegation was false; it means only that the diocese or religious order could not determine whether the alleged abuse actually took place'. Consequently there is a potential rogue 30 per cent floating through the various statistics.

The Review Board are on much firmer ground when they share the fruits of their interviews, including those conducted with many of the hierarchy of the US Catholic Church. They record how prior to 2002

'the Vatican had refrained from assuming a significant role with respect to the response of the bishops in the United States to allegations of sexual abuse of minors by members of the clergy. The Vatican did not recognise the scope or the gravity of the problem facing the Church in the United States despite numerous warning signs; and it rebuffed earlier attempts to reform procedures for removing predator priests.'

The report then gives a detailed account of how 'a number of influential bishops in the United States' beginning in the late 1980s asked the Vatican to create a fast-track process for removing sexually abusing priests because the process under Canon Law was a long-drawn-out affair which at every turn was designed to protect the accused priest even after he had been found guilty. The process also required 'the participation of the victim. A number of bishops, concerned in part that victims would find it traumatising to address their abuser in a formal proceeding, were reluctant to ask for their assistance.' In this way, concern for the victim protected the abuser. There were repeated and continuous requests by the bishops for a fast-track process 'throughout the 1990s but again to no avail'.

Eventually even the arch-procrastinator John Paul II had accepted that he had to take some form of action. In 1993 he set up a committee to study how best Canon Law could be applied to 'the particular situation in the United States', for till his dying day he still believed that the sexual abuse by Catholic clergy is 'a uniquely American problem'.

The Heads of the various Vatican Congregations; close friends and colleagues like Cardinal Ratzinger; the numerous papal nuncios around the world: any or all of them could have told the Pope the truth. He could have had the various religious orders investigated – the Salesians or the Franciscans, for example. Both have been operating a global version of the secret system for decades. They move sexually abusing priests from Latin America to Europe, from Asia to Africa.

He could have recalled the United States bishops to the Vatican and demanded to know why so many of their number were determined to stop the National Review Board from doing the very job that the bishops created it to do, namely ensure that every bishop in the United States is subjected to a yearly national audit to ensure the dioceses are complying with the official policies on clerical sexual abuse. He might have asked his bishops just what it is they are so frightened of the Review Board uncovering.

With the first round of reports in, the noted critic Father Andrew Greeley observed in March 2004, 'The Catholic Left would have us believe that the most serious problem the Church faces is clerical celibacy. The Catholic Right, on the other hand, wants to blame everything on homosexuals.' Father Greeley backs neither. For him:

'the guilty people are the bishops – insensitive, cowardly, ignorant, clericalist – who reassigned such priests [i.e. sexual abusers]. Equally guilty are their staffs – vicars general, vicars for the clergy, civil and canon lawyers, psychiatrists, chiefs of Catholic mental institutions.'

It is a long list but as the National Review report powerfully illustrates there are quite a number of the 'guilty' missing.

The Review Board had concluded that 90 per cent of the nearly 200 Catholic dioceses within the United States were 'in compliance with the pledge that the Bishops had made in mid 2002 to better protect children and punish offenders'. But victim support groups dismissed the report as biased. One such group, SNAP (Survivors Network of those Abused by Priests) revealed that only two of its nearly five thousand members were invited to speak to the investigators. Far more significantly the bishops had recommended to the investigators whom they should interview. As for those archdioceses which had failed to comply, New York and Omaha were two. 'There is no mechanism to sanction church officials who do not comply . . .'

A similar Alice-in-Wonderland situation still prevails within the Roman Catholic Church in England and Wales. For all the fine words of the original Nolan reports, in July 2004 the latest annual report revealed that during 2003 there had been sixty complaints of sexual, physical and emotional abuse and that as of mid-2004 not one of the alleged abusers had been prosecuted. The continued use of the secret system was demonstrated to parishioners in Kentish Town, north London, when they learned in late 2004 that for the past two years a paedophile priest, Father William Hofton, had been ministering to their spiritual needs. The truth came to light only when Hofton was charged with sexually abusing a further two young boys.

He pleaded guilty and was sentenced to four years' imprisonment.

Back in the United States, fall-out from the scandal continued to emerge. In May 2004 it was announced that the Boston archdiocese would be closing at least one sixth of its parishes, churches and schools. Cardinal O'Malley was insistent that the closures were not linked to the huge payout of over $100 million to sexual abuse victims. In fiscal terms perhaps he was right but the scandal has stripped the Catholic Church in the United States of much of its prestige and trust and that has been reflected with empty pews.

In July the Archdiocese of Portland became the first Catholic diocese to file for bankruptcy. The diocese having already paid out more than $50 million was faced with further claims totalling over $150 million. The bankruptcy hearing under 'Chapter 11' protects essential assets and temporarily halts any ongoing litigation.

During the summer of 2004, Austria was rocked with a second clerical sex scandal involving a good friend of the Pope's. Bishop Kurt Krenn, a leading supporter of the paedophile Cardinal Groer, was accused of condoning a wide range of sexual activities that were occurring within a seminary that was under his control. The offences included possession of child pornography, downloading vast quantities of obscene material from a Polish web site, sexual abuse of seminarians by priests and overwhelming evidence of the existence of a homosexual network. Bishop Krenn refused to resign and dismissed the various activities as 'childish pranks'. With Austria yet again plunged into an uproar because of clerical sexual abuse, the Vatican prevaricated. Eventually an Apostolic Visitator-Investigator was sent from Rome and after yet more closed-door discussions, Bishop Krenn reluctantly resigned.

In 2002 the American bishops had also been promised a

visit from an Apostolic Visitator. Three years later he had still to put in an appearance, yet the scandals in the US continued to emerge. In September the former bishop of Springfield, Massachusetts, Thomas Dupre, was charged on two counts with child rape. Subsequently the county district attorney said that although he was satisfied the offences had been commited he would not prosecute because the charges fell outside the statute of limitations. The same month, across the country in California, fresh indictments were filed in court. The papers detail thirty-one priests who are alleged to have sexually abused sixty-three children in Santa Barbara County. The victims include three girls who were repeatedly assaulted inside the San Roque confessional on Saturday afternoons between 1979 and 1981. The entire litany of alleged offences covers a period from the 1930s to the 1990s.

In Kentucky a class action with some 200 alleged victims is currently in mediation. In Tucson, Arizona, in the face of nineteen civil lawsuits alleging sexual abuse by 126 of the diocesan priests, the local bishop, Gerald Kicanas, is preparing to declare the diocese bankrupt. The legal actions have been brought on behalf of over 100 people. The bishop has already overseen the paying out of nearly $20 million. In mid-2004 Pope John Paul II defrocked two of the Tucson priests, Teta and Robert Trupia. The latter was described by Bishop Kicanas as a 'notorious and serially sexual' predator. Teta had been suspended by the diocese in 2002 after being the subject of 'credible accusations of child abuse'. In December 2004 the diocese of Orange County, California, agreed a settlement of $100 million to be paid to eighty-seven victims. Next up is Los Angeles, the nation's largest diocese, facing over 500 claims. During the same month, the Archdiocese of Louisville agreed to pay out $27.7 million and the Archdiocese of Chicago agreed to pay out $12 million.

I asked Father Doyle to estimate just how many cases are currently working their way through the legal process within the United States.

'I would say probably close to 2,000 and there are still more coming up. You know, what you also have are the orphanages and schools where the kid victims are coming forward. It is a never-ending process. And I along with others who are deeply involved believe we are nowhere near the end of it. Nowhere near cleaning up the garbage and the depth and breadth of the abuse.'

Hard on the heels of Father Doyle's grim predictions came confirmation. In February 2005 a criminal investigation was opened in Dallas by the district attorney. Three years after the Dallas diocese had claimed that all allegations of clerical abuse had been reported, new revelations indicated the diocese had suppressed information on additional cases. The same week, Archbishop Daniel Pilarczyk of Cincinnati was exposed for the second time as protecting a serial sexual abuser. Father David Kelley abused dozens of boys and was able to continue his assaults over many years because of the effectiveness of the secret system that operated in Cincinnati. Pilarczyk, it will be remembered, was one of the bishops who had been so dismissive of the 1985 report written by Father Doyle, Father Peterson and lawyer Ray Mouton. He was also the bishop who in November 2003 had been obliged to admit in open court that his archdiocese had 'knowingly failed' to report to the relevant authorities a string of clerical sexual abuse cases.

Within a few days of this latest scandal in Cincinnati, the results of the second yearly audit of sex-abuse prevention policies in American dioceses were published. It revealed that 1,092 new claims were filed against clergy in 2004 and that more than $840 million had been paid out in legal settlements since 1950. Again it must be emphasised that the compensation figure is dismissed by many as being a serious under-estimate. By early June after the announcement that the diocese of Covington, Kentucky, was to pay out $120 million, the official figure of compensation paid stood at $1.06 billion. In Southern California alone, lawyers acting for abuse victims have insisted that, when their various cases have been resolved, additional payments will add a futher $1 billion. The spiralling cost of the compensation claims is a crisis that is not confined to the United States. It exists in many countries. In late March 2005, for example, the Catholic Church in Ireland was facing further claims over the next five years that one estimate put at £35 million.

In August 2005, the Portland litigation took several more bizarre directions. Every one of the nearly 400,000 Roman Catholics in the west coast state of Oregon were advised that they were defendants in the case and the man who had succeeded Cardinal Ratzinger as Head of the Congregation for the Doctrine of the Faith, Archbishop Levada, was named as a defendant. He had previously been Archbishop of Portland. Levada, having waived diplomatic immunity, agreed to be examined under oath in January 2006. The naming of Levada as a defendant was not without an ironic aspect. The Archbishop had early access to the detailed report of Fathers Doyle and Peterson and Ray Mouton in 1985 and after initial enthusiasm for the recommendations it contained had been one of those who allowed the report to wither on the vine. By 2005 abuse victims in Portland had already had judgement against the diocese amounting to over $150 million. Dozens of other plaintiffs are seeking $400 million in pending lawsuits.

During the last week of September 2005, the Apostolic Visitation, an official inspection of every one of the 229

Catholic seminaries in the United States agreed upon in April 2002, finally began. That it took over three years to commence is an eloquent comment on Vatican priorities.

In October, the Ferns Report was published in Ireland, revealing for the first time the extent of clerical sexual abuse over many decades. It was also the story of physical cruelty, neglect and incompetence, compounded by criminal conspiracy, corruption and arrogance by men unfit to be priests. There was Bishop Donal Herlihy, for twenty years in charge of Ferns, a man who refused to treat the issue of sexual abuse as a criminal matter, regarding it as a moral issue. Then there was his successor, Bishop Brendan Comiskey, who consistently failed to remove clerical abusers because he considered that to do so would be 'unjust', since the allegations of abuse were not substantiated.

The Ferns scandal opened the floodgates in Ireland. Not a day went by it seemed without further revelations up and down the country, from Cork and Ross in the south to Derry and Down and Connor in Northern Ireland. It was revealed that over the past forty years, 241 priests had been accused of sexual abuse. Twenty-two had been convicted but many had died before trial. In November, the Irish Government announced an in-depth probe in the Dublin diocese in response to allegations of sexual abuse against sixty-seven Dublin priests. Subsequently Justice Minister McDowell announced that an independent investigation would take place within every diocese in the country.

A week after the Dublin revelations, police in North Yorkshire revealed that they had concluded a fifteen-month investigation into years of sexual abuse by English clerics. The location stunned not only devout Catholics but also much of the nation. Ampleforth College, England's most celebrated Catholic public school, has as its mission the 'spiritual, moral and intellectual' education of children who will 'become inspired by high ideals and capable of leadership'. For at least three decades, between 1966 and 1995, pupils were also at high risk of sexual abuse by some of the monks who taught there. The assaults ranged from minor abuse to rape. There were at least thirty to forty victims but the ultimate number of victims during that period has been estimated by former pupils to be 'in three figures'. Some of the victims at the prep school were under ten years of age. During those years, Cardinal Basil Hume was Abbot of Ampleforth and the Archbishop of Westminster, the Primate of England. Three of the paedophile priests have been before the courts; three others died before their abuses of the children became known. Cardinal Hume covered up the activities of Father Piers Grant-Ferris. These included sexually abusing fifteen boys over a nine-year period. The cardinal also offered a woman who had been molested by another priest an unsolicited £1,500 'donation' towards counselling while urging her not to contact the police. There is no doubt that the Primate would have been forced to resign his office if these facts had become public knowledge before his death in 1997. Cardinal Hume's motive has a familiar ring: 'For the good of mother church.'

In the United States, a federal judge in Kentucky has recently ruled that the Holy See is a foreign state that enjoys certain immunity protections. In the judge's opinion these included protection for the Vatican against any claims arising from sexual abuse litigation: immunity from not only criminal prosecution but any form of legal action with regard to the clerical abuse of children. In December 2005 another federal judge, this time in Texas, ruled that Pope Benedict XVI enjoys immunity as a Head of State and removed him from a civil lawsuit accusing him of conspiracy to cover up sexual abuse of minors by a seminarian.

If 2005 had finished on a positive note for the Pope and his colleagues within the Vatican, they would have taken little comfort from the news coming out of Boston during the first weeks of the New Year. It was revealed that in the past two years alone the Archdiocese of Boston had received more than $215 million from insurance and land sales, enough to pay alleged victims of clergy abuse twenty-eight times the compensation that the Archdiocese has offered. Simultaneously it was revealed that 200 new claims have been made by alleged victims against the Archdiocese. By March 2006 the official 'audit' for US dioceses for the previous year reinforced the belief that clerical sexual abuse continued to be the biggest problem confronting the Church. There had been 783 credible new accusations of sexual abuse against American clerics lodged that year, 81 per cent involving male victims. The American dioceses paid out in compensation nearly half a billion dollars, $466.9 million. This represents an increase of nearly 300 per cent over the 2004 figure of $157.8 million. The Church paid out a further $13 million to support offending priests.

Also in March 2006 the results of an investigation by Archbishop Martin into clerical paedophiles within the Dublin diocese were revealed. Over one hundred priests had been accused over a period reaching back to 1940. The Archbishop observed, 'It's hard for me to see that in some of these cases, so many children were abused. It's very hard to weigh that up against anything.' The diocese has already paid out some $10 million and like so many of its American counterparts faced selling property to meet further compensation claims.

The global backlog of cases is now so great that any bishop writing to the CDF seeking a decision on an errant priest faces an eighteen-month delay before he will get a response. On top of this caseload the now Cardinal Levada has continuing problems of his own. Among the unresolved issues in Levada's former diocese of Portland are allegations that he applied the secret system personally, including secret payments to victims and allowing a self-confessed paedophile to continue working in a number of parishes.

In May 2006, *The Power and the Glory* was first published in Italy, after the allegations contained within this section regarding Father Marcial Maciel, the founder of the Legionaries of Christ, reached a resolution. The enquiry that the then Cardinal Ratzinger had ordered and then suspended 'to spare the Holy Father any embarrasment' had been reactivated. Cardinal Levada and Pope Benedict XVI had concluded that at least some of the allegations were well-founded. Why it had taken decades to reach this conclusion was not explained. A group of men who had been systematically abused over many years, and vilified when they sought Vatican recognition of what they had suffered, had finally achieved a small measure of the justice they so richly deserved. The late Pope John Paul II, who was fully aware of the detailed evidence against Maciel, had responded with words of praise for the paedophile and honoured the man. His successor, who refused to act during Wojtyla's lifetime, has finally approved Levada's decision to remove Maciel from priestly ministry and to order him to spend the remaining days of his life in 'penitence and prayer'. He was to be spared a canonical trial because of 'his advanced age and delicate health'.

The Vatican that for centuries has told people on pain of eternal damnation how they should lead their sexual lives now demands that the clerical sexual abuses that have been revealed over the last thirty years should be forgiven and forgotten. Pope John Paul II, Cardinal Ratzinger and a great many other like-minded Princes of the Church are on public record claiming that it is the abusers who are the victims. To quote Cardinal Ratzinger:

'It has to do with the reflection of our highly sexualized society. Priests are also affected by the general situation. They may be especially vulnerable, or susceptible, although the percentage of abuse cases is no higher than in other occupations. One would naturally expect it to be lower . . .'

For Cardinal Norberto Carrera of Mexico, the villains of the story were not the sex-abusing clergy, but the *New York Times*, the *Boston Globe*, the *Washington Post* and any other media outlets that sought out the truth about Cardinal Law of Boston. Their activities resembled for Carrera 'what happened in the past century with persecutions in Mexico, in Spain, in Nazi Germany and in communist countries'. Prelates in many countries have expressed similar sentiments. Those who expose the sex abusers are denounced as 'enemies of the Church'. Demonstrably, the Catholic Church's concept of zero tolerance is to apply it to its critics while offering maximum tolerance and understanding to the criminals within its ranks.

By the failure not only of Pope John Paul II and his successor but also of virtually the entire Catholic hierarchy to confront the issue of sexual abuse within the clergy, the Catholic Church has abdicated any historic rights it has previously claimed to speak to her laity on the issues of faith and morals. To abuse a child, to violate an innocent, is for the vast majority an act beyond belief. For a member of the priesthood or a religious order to abuse a child, an adolescent or adult is the ultimate betrayal of trust. The damage may be eventually sublimated, but it is permanent. Clerical sex abuse is a total attack on the body, mind and soul of the victim. It combines physical pain, mental anguish, and emotional and spiritual rape.

Part 2: Ratzinger: Confronting the Secret System

THE SPIN DOCTORS WORKING on behalf of the US Catholic bishops continued to be kept fully occupied as confirmed by just a few examples from the National Review Board's press releases covering 2007. In the United States during that year a further 689 victims made 691 allegations. These are referred to as 'old cases'. While most of the victims were young boys aged between ten and fourteen, no exact breakdown was ever forthcoming. The financial figure for settlements for that year is quoted as $420 million, not including attorneys' fees of $53.4 million; therapy for the victims at $7.2 million; support for offenders at $13.3 million and $4.3 million for 'other costs'. Thus the total cost for the dioceses in the United States for the year 2007 was $498 million – just short of half a billion dollars. To that figure should be added the costs borne by the religious institutes. When those various sums are included, the combined cost to dioceses, eparchies and religious institutes is $615 million.

This masking of the real financial damage being done to the US Catholic Church as a direct result of clerical sexual abuse of the young continued into the following year. The National Review Board's report for 2008 includes the following statement:

'The total allegation-related expenditures by Dioceses, eparchies and clerical and mixed religious institutes decreased by 29 per cent between 2007 and 2008 . . . In 2008 the amount paid in settlements was a total of $374,408,554.'

In fact, the combined total – when the legal fees and the other factors referred to earlier are included – was $436.1 million, a total for the two years of $1.511 billion.

The US bishops were not alone in displaying an ability to be economical with the truth. In a great many countries unacceptable behaviour was being exposed. In Ireland, one fall from grace was particularly surprising. It featured Bishop John Magee, a priest who formerly had been secretary to three popes, the third being Pope John Paul II. Magee was a man who knew the ways of Vatican City State intimately. Promoted to bishop by the Pope in 1987, he returned to his native Ireland to assume the pastoral care of some 120,000 souls in the Diocese of Cloyne.

A number of Vaticanologists, a breed of journalist that takes pride in being in front of the media pack, were sure that Bishop Magee was being groomed for high office. They foresaw him becoming Archbishop of Armagh, followed by the award of a cardinal's red hat. It was not to be. Perhaps a man who has spent many years very close to the supreme power of the Catholic Church unconsciously assumes attitudes and a demeanour of a position higher than reality justifies.

Initially, Bishop Magee's activities were very successful but eventually his manner began to jar. There had been a high of nearly fifty seminarians in the diocese but the number began to dwindle. By the latter part of the first decade of the twenty-first century there were just three young men training for the priesthood.

Bishop Magee demonstrated a constant concern over the issue of clerical abuse. Writing in a pastoral letter in April 2002, he declared that clerical abuse of children had caused 'great pain and shame to the whole church in Ireland. A sacred trust had been betrayed and innocent young people have been hurt and violated in a most heinous way by priests.' He wrote that the process of healing could only be effective 'when the full truth is told'. He continued, 'I fully endorse the decision of the Irish bishops to order an independent audit of all diocesan files to establish the full truth about how complaints regarding child sexual abuse had been dealt with.'

At the time that Magee made these commendable observations, the Ferns investigation referred to earlier had begun its work. By January 2005, the commission was in its final stages. Again Bishop Magee was the bearer of positive news on the issue of clerical sexual abuse of the young. He informed the new Diocesan Council of Priests that he had appointed a full-time coordinator within the Diocesan Child Protection Committee to train everyone involved in ministry with children. More than 150 priests, religious and laity had already been trained, and Magee continued, 'I look toward a much healthier and more secure environment in Church-related activities.'

In October 2005, the ticking time bomb that was the Ferns Report was published, with over 100 allegations of sexual abuse by twenty-one priests identified. The attacks occurred between 1962 and 2002. The most recent took place at virtually the same time that the Ferns Commission had begun its investigation.

The publication of the Ferns Report stimulated Bishop Magee to pick up his pen again. His letter on child protection was read aloud at masses throughout the Cloyne Diocese. It contained the following statement:

'Words of apology appear very weak and inadequate
and yet cannot be left unspoken. Our first concern
must be to reach out to victims and to ensure that what
has happened will never happen again.'

Bishop Magee's various utterances regarding clerical abuse
of children clearly indicate a man totally committed to full
disclosure of such abuses that were brought to his attention.
They reveal a bishop, as early as April 2002, in full accord
with the belief 'that the full truth must be told' and that 'the
decision of his fellow Irish bishops that there should be an
independent audit of all Diocesan files to establish the full
truth about how complaints of child sexual abuse had been
dealt with' was the only way forward. Total transparency.

In fact, Bishop Magee's domain of Cloyne was the only
diocese in the entire country not to follow the child protection procedures that had been brought in by the bishops in
1996. These guidelines were updated in 2000 and again in
2005. Through this entire period Magee failed to practise
what he had regularly preached.

In December 2004, a priest reported to Bishop Magee
that he had been abused as a child, at that time he declined
to identify the assailant. In May 2005, he named his abuser,
who was another priest of the diocese. Four months later
Magee met the perpetrator, who subsequently resigned. Six
months after this the Gardaí (Irish police) were informed;
only the name of the victim was given. The fact that the
accused was a fellow priest in the diocese was suppressed.
The 1996 guidelines call for immediate full disclosure to the
civil authorities. In Magee's domain this case was far from
being unique. A second priest merely referred to in official
reports as Father B had caused a string of complaints to be
made to the bishop.

The first allegation against Father B was made in 1995 by
the father of a young girl. The police were informed. A

second allegation was made in September 1996, by the mother of a teenage boy. On 9 December 1997, another girl alleged she had been sexually abused by Father B while he heard her confession. The priest, a career guidance teacher, was placed on restrictive ministry by the bishop. In January 2003, the mother of the teenage boy was back in Magee's office, complaining that there had been further assaults on her son by the same priest.

The first time that the police authorities were informed of these allegations was more than eight years after the initial complaint. The report of the subsequent investigation by the National Board for Safeguarding Children (NBSC) on behalf of the Catholic Church makes it clear that Bishop Magee and his colleagues' 'failure to name the alleged perpetrator to the Gardaí was not exceptional. Indeed, it is described as "their normal practice" by the Bishop in a signed minute of a meeting that took place on 25 May 2006.' The investigation also found 'glaringly absent any references to the need to protect vulnerable people and to act in a timely and effective way to achieve this end'. The only concern appeared to be for the alleged abusing priest.

So, for a number of years stretching over two decades there was not one Church policy regarding clerical sexual abuse of children, but two. The first applied to the entire country, with one exception. The second applied exclusively to the Diocese of Cloyne and the manner that its bishop managed affairs for the 120,000 residents. Confronted with the evidence that had been so painstakingly researched by NBSC officials, Bishop Magee's response was: 'the safety of children is the priority for me and the Diocese of Cloyne.'

The appalling damage that Magee and his colleagues perpetrated within Cloyne was not confined to that one diocese. The revelations came at a time when many within the country were hoping that, with the various checks that had been implemented by the Church, they had perhaps turned the corner, that the worst was behind them.

Confronted with the implications of the NSBC report, Bishop Magee faced a great many calls for his immediate removal, ideally his resignation. The bishop, however, declined to oblige. Magee, who had been at the very heart of the Catholic Church's supreme power base for decades, failed to grasp the fact that, as of January 2009, he was devoid of official support. Finally, on 7 March 2009, he announced that at his request the Pope had placed the running of the diocese in the hands of Dermot Clifford, Metropolitan Archbishop of Cashel and Emly. On 24 March 2010, it was announced by the Holy See that Bishop Magee had formally resigned from his duties as Bishop of Cloyne and was now bishop emeritus.

After a report from the Health Service Executive was published, detailing a number of other cases that had not been reported to the authorities or dealt with according to self-regulatory procedures within Magee's diocese, there were yet further demands for the removal of the bishop. His response was to apologise to the victims of these abuses. He also indicated that he had no intention of resigning. The damage to the image of the faith in Ireland continued to mount. Finally it was announced during Easter 2010 that Pope Benedict XVI had accepted the resignation of Bishop John Magee of Cloyne.

What had made the events in Cloyne particularly shocking was not the number of cases of sexual abuse; in truth the numbers to date are mercifully small. What really hit home was the involvement of such a highly respected man at the centre of this scandal. John Magee had been widely considered to be an example of the very best of Irish priesthood. Long before his fate was determined there was a widespread apprehension that if someone like Magee could 'get it so wrong', then what did it say about other bishops in Ireland?

Long before the departure of Magee, Ireland had its answer to that question.

The Ferns Report of 2005 had given part of the answer and more devastating revelations were to follow, and not only in Ireland.

The disreputable career of the Reverend Marcial Maciel Delgollado founder superior general of the Order of the Legionaries of Christ continued unhindered throughout the pontificate of Pope John Paul II. Founded in 1941, the Legion of Christ was declared by Maciel to have a very specific mission: 'to extend the Kingdom of Christ in society . . . Our fundamental mission is to bring all people to know love and share Christ with others, with Apostolates and institutions in the fields of education, service to the poor and evangelization'. The then Cardinal Ratzinger who, as the head of the congregation, was charged with the responsibility of bringing not only paedophiles but all forms of sexually abusing priests to book, took no action whatsoever against the paedophile Maciel between 1982 and 2006, other than to observe to one of my Vatican informants that he had secretly ordered the inquiry into volumes of sworn affidavits detailing facts of sexual abuse by Maciel over more than half a century, 'to spare the Holy Father any embarrassment'.

Pope John Paul II went to meet his maker on Saturday, 2 April 2005. Thanks to the then Cardinal Ratzinger, he had indeed been spared any embarrassment with regard to the activities of Marcial Maciel Delgollado. It is unlikely that even if he had been confronted with the full-unvarnished truth that he would have accepted any of it. Years earlier he had personally ignored sworn affidavits from a number of Maciel's victims. He had protected active paedophiles such as Cardinal Groer and Father Maciel for many years. It was a protection that included rounding angrily on the accusers of the founders of the Legion of Christ, and describing Maciel as 'an efficacious guide to youth'.

With Karol Wojtyla dead, and Ratzinger elected as his successor, one might expect some rapid action from the Vatican. After all the new Pope had privately expressed the view years earlier that the evidence against Maciel was overwhelming, which is hardly surprising when one realises that testimony on Maciel had also been sent through official Vatican channels in 1976, 1978 and 1989. Finally, in 2007 the Vatican announced that after an intensive examination of the various accusations and 'taking account of the advanced age of the Reverend Maciel and his delicate health it had decided to refrain from taking any action against Maciel'. Instead he had been invited by the new Prefect of the Congregation of the Faith, Cardinal William Levada, to 'a reserved life of prayer and penance, renouncing very public ministry'.

Presumably, that is an example of the Vatican version of 'zero tolerance' and there Pope Benedict devoutely hoped the matter had been laid to rest. The Reverend Maciel died the following year on 30 January 2008. Many people must have breathed a collective sigh of relief, If so, they were premature.

In less than a month further evidence began to emerge that Maciel, apart from his persistent and continuous abuse of young boys entrusted to his care, had also indulged in sexual affairs with women. A daughter, now a thirty-year-old woman, emerged from her comfortable middle-class life in Madrid where she owned a number of residential properties, courtesy of her kind father, who had supplied the funds – originally part of donations made to the Legion of Christ. A former chief financial officer of the Legion, Father Fitcher, revealed that he routinely gave Maciel large sums of cash and that no accounting was ever made. Ten thousand dollars at a time would vanish. Maciel's followers, meanwhile, would have to account for every cent they spent. Father Fitcher may not have known where this money was going but it is inconceivable that every senior member was equally unaware.

The Legionaries of Christ was not a hole-in-the-corner cult comprising a mere handful of followers. At the time of its founder's death in January 2008, it claimed to have over 700 priests and 2,000 seminarians in twenty countries. Estimates of its assets varied: the Italian newsweekly, *L'Espresso*, considered the Legion to be worth €25 billion; the *Wall Street Journal* stated that the Order's annual budget was $650 million.

Other costs that the founder had met concerned his life-long addiction to morphine. Among his many admirers, it has been alleged, were quite a number who benefited financially if not spiritually. Three of his strongest supporters over the years who allegedly received substantial payments were Vatican Secretary of State from 1990 to 2006, Cardinal Angelo Sodano; Cardinal Eduardo Martinez Somalo, prefect of the Congregation for Institutes of Consecrated Life and Societies of Apostolic Life and Monsignor Stanislaw Dziwisz, now Cardinal Dziwisz, for many years Pope John Paul II's personal secretary. When the *National Catholic Reporter* 'sought repeatedly' to contact and interview the three cardinals before running an extensive two-part series on the life and times of Maciel it was met with blanket refusals and evasion, which is strange in view of the fact that acceptance of such monies by the three men would not, in itself, contravene any Church law: a large cash donation of this nature would be seen as 'a pious gift'.

Senior members of the Legion declared shortly after Maciel's death that they were certain that the founder's soul had gone directly to Heaven. The overwhelming factual evidence suggests the contrary direction. If there is indeed a life after this one that conforms to the version that the Catholic faith teaches, then surely this malevolent man's soul will be a long way from paradise. The act of sacramentally forgiving an individual he had just abused is itself a profound abuse of the confessional; it was but one of many acts that put the founder of the Legion beyond the pale. It is a blasphemy that Maciel perpetrated on hundreds of occasions.

Pope Benedict has the task – one of many with regard to clerical sexual abuse – of resolving whether or not to dissolve the Legionaries of Christ. It is self-evident to a great many that he undoubtedly should take that step. To do less, to allow the Legion to continue in some sanitised form, would be to abuse again every single victim of Maciel. Despite the overwhelming evidence, there are people out there arguing and lobbying for the continuation of the Legion 'under new management'. They talk of 'the great good' that still exists within the Legion. Would any parent of a young child take a chance on that?

The current regime controlling the Legion – a regime that assured the world that Maciel's soul was now residing in Heaven, and that to cast doubt on the assertions that Maciel had throughout his life been 'a living saint' was an act of wickedness – defies belief. Less than a year after Maciel's death in January 2008, those defenders of Maciel were obliged to admit that their 'living saint' was in fact the opposite. Later in 2009, senior members of the Legion were apologising to 'all who have been harmed or scandalised by the "misdeeds" of Father Marcial Maciel,' and regretting their own 'shortcomings of communication', Legion-speak for lies. The temporary leadership also acknowledged that the now former 'living saint' had fathered a child during a long affair, 'and committed other grave acts'.

For more than sixty years Father Maciel had been held up as an exemplar of virtue by, among others, Father Maciel himself and Pope John Paul II. By March 2010, the executive concluded, 'We accept that given the gravity of his faults, we cannot take his person as a model of Christian or priestly life.' This statement coincided with the report of five bishops who, acting on the Pope's instructions, had been investigating the Legion. It also happened at around the same time as a Mexican woman, Blanca Lara Guitierrez, revealed that Father Maciel was the father of two of her children. It transpired that they had remained ignorant for many years that their father was a priest.

Among those Legion members who have been aware for some years of the nature and acts of their leader is the second ranking official of the order, Father Luis Carza Medina; there are others. In an internal memorandum of May 2010, the current leaders of the Legion demonstrated that the mendacity that was such a feature of Maciel's life lives on among the Legion's current leadership. They now assert that they knew nothing of the double life of their founder. This is a position that is contradicted by the realities of significant evidence as well as plain common sense. The current leadership, like Maciel, has been weighed in the balance and found wanting.

During the past two years Pope Benedict has been subjected to global criticism over the issue of clerical sexual abuse. To dissolve the Legionaries of Christ and to declare the Reverend Marcial Maciel and his sect anathema would be a powerful statement that the clean-up had finally begun of this filth that permeates virtually every country in the world where there is a significant Roman Catholic population.

It is not going to happen under this Pope who, as Cardinal Ratzinger, the Prefect of the Congregation for the Doctrine of the Faith (CDF), earned over the years a number of other titles, including Vatican Enforcer. The list of some of the Catholic Church's finest scholars and thinkers who were silenced and permanently damaged by Ratzinger during his years at the CDF is lengthy. Their crime was to hold and express opinions that were unacceptable, in the minds of Pope John Paul II and his enforcer. Karol Wojtyla not only expected unquestioning acceptance of his authority, he demanded it. The man who ensured that the papal demand was met was Ratzinger.

Clifford Longley, editorial consultant for the *Tablet* and long-time internationally respected religious affairs author and journalist, observed, 'Cardinal Ratzinger is disliked and feared throughout the Catholic world.' This is not the case anymore; that was a lifetime ago. A decision is awaited from the Pope on the fate of the Legion and its members. Every man protests not merely innocence but also total ignorance of the activities of the late leader. Today, the Legion is an empire of universities (fifteen at the last count), schools, commercial businesses, the fifty institutes of higher learning, the 176 elementary and secondary schools, with the current number of students approaching 135,000. Easier far easier, Pope Benedict will probably reason, to leave the existing infrastructures relatively untouched, dropping the name Legionaries of Christ.

The name change could possibly be announced by the apostolic delegate that the Pope will undoubtedly appoint. It is already beginning to look as if an attempt will be made to paint the late founder into a corner – a one-man band of corruption. Those among the rank and file should take great care with this particular gambit; no religious order in the history of the Catholic Church has ever survived after repudiating its founder.

Those advising the Pope on this entire issue are very conscious of the need to proceed with caution on the various problems outlined above, particularly the wealth of the Legion – not only the current fortune but also future donations. Among the most prominent donors over the years are the owners of the Mexican breadmaking empire Grupo Bimbo, and Carlos Slim, the telecoms magnate listed by *Forbes* as the world's wealthiest man. An indication of the kind of money some of these donors have given in the past can be gauged by the sums reputed to have been given to the Order by Flora Barragan de Garza, who is believed to have donated $50 million during her lifetime. The size of the scandal that has now been generated could see such donations finding a new home, unless it is handled with exquisite finesse.

One of Father Maciel's children, Jose Raul Gonzalez, is currently preparing to sue the Legionaries of Christ, claiming fraud and negligence. The Vatican in general and Pope Benedict in particular would be seriously damaged if that action proceeds.

While the saga of the Legionaries has continued apace other scandals in different locations have also demanded attention. The Legion is not an isolated aberration. The long Lent for the Irish Church also appears to have no end in sight. Well before the enforced removal of Bishop Magee, the Irish Government was announcing plans to expand a probe into Church treatment of sexual abuse complaints. The fall-out from the Ferns Report of 2005 was still resonating four years later. One of the most positive results occurred when more than 70 per cent of the priests in the Diocese of Ferns volunteered to submit to police background checks. Public confidence in Ferns might have been further restored if the other 30 per cent had followed that lead.

In April 2009, Archbishop Diarmuid Martin of Dublin publicly warned all Irish Catholics to brace themselves for the publication of the Ryan Report in May. This was a monumental investigation, named after Chairperson Judge Sean Ryan, begun in 1999 and concluded ten years later. Entitled 'The Report of the Commission on Child Sexual Abuse', it dealt in great detail within its 2,600 pages with clerical abuse reaching back to before the Second World

War. The Commission's brief was to investigate all forms of child abuse in Irish institutions for children. The majority of allegations it investigated focused upon the system operated in some sixty residential 'Reformatory and Industrial Schools' operated by Catholic Church Orders, more often than not run by the Christian Brothers

The report should be made compulsory reading for the wide range of apologists not only for the current Pope, it is a truly shocking indictment. The report establishes that the system within these schools treated children 'like prison inmates and slaves' devoid of any legal rights. The report identified sub-human behaviour that repeatedly records beatings and rapes, subjection to naked beatings in public, being forced to perform oral sex, and even beatings after failed rape attempts by Christian Brothers.

Adjectives including 'systemic', 'pervasive', 'chronic', 'excessive', 'arbitrary' and 'endemic' are used by the Commission to describe the indescribable. Those apologists will search in vain for evidence that what occurred was perpetrated by a very small minority, although even one perverted degenerate would be one too many. It is clear from the details contained within this document that we are confronted with a widespread evil that went on year after year, decade after decade.

It is mystifying therefore that the late Karol Wojtyla dismissed the clerical abuse of children as 'an American problem'. Anyone who shares that level of self-delusion and therefore concludes, for example, that what confronted the Ryan Commission was first 'an Irish problem' should reflect that wherever the Christian Brothers went – be it Canada, Australia or elsewhere – they brought with them their version of Christianity, which included systematic brutality. The report contains forty-three conclusions and twenty recommendations. The former include:

• *Overall*: physical and emotional abuse and neglect were

features of the institutions. Sexual abuse occurred in many of them, particularly boys' institutions. Schools were run in a severe regimented manner that imposed unreasonable and oppressive discipline on children and even on staff.

• *Physical abuse*: the Reformatory and Industrial Schools depended on rigid control by means of severe corporal punishment and fear of such punishment, which permeated more of the institutions and most of those run for boys. Children lived with the daily terror of not knowing where the next beating was coming from.

• *Sexual abuse*: sexual abuse was endemic in boys' institutions. The schools investigated revealed a substantial level of sexual abuse of boys in care that extended from improper touching and fondling to rape with violence. Perpetrators of abuse were able to operate undetected for long periods at the core of institutions.

When confronted with evidence of sexual abuse, the religious authorities' response was to transfer the offender to another location where, in many instances, he was free to abuse again. Although girls were subjected to predatory sexual abuse, it was not systemic in girls' schools. There is a belief in some circles that this secret system of moving a molester is a gambit that began in the 1980s, but the long reach of this investigation, back to testimony that is pre-Second World War, exposes this canard. The evidence extends much further and ranges from 1914 onwards.

Over 25,000 children attended these institutions. Approximately 1,500 came forward with complaints to the Commission. Doubtless that number would have been far greater if others had lived to tell their tale; still others did not testify for a variety of reasons, ranging from shame to fear. The effect of these abuses upon the children is there for the rest of their lives. It was not easy for any of them to testify to strangers; that would take extraordinary courage. They talked of the neglect, the poor standards of physical care, of the gnawing hunger day after day, struggling to survive with minimal food that was inedible and badly prepared. They described the lack of heating in bleak rooms, and the emotional as well as the physical abuse. Going to the toilet would often be seized upon as an opportunity for degradation and humiliation. They recalled that the criticism was incessant, as was the verbal abuse, which was invariably accompanied with shouting of how worthless they were.

The Commission also established that successive governments had conspired with the perpetrators. The Department of Education inspections were 'fundamentally flawed and incapable of being effective'. The department did not apply the standards laid out in the rules and their own guidelines when investigating complaints but 'sought to protect and defend the religious congregations and schools'. The department dealt inadequately with complaints about sexual abuse, 'which were generally dismissed or ignored'.

The Commission's recommendations were limited by the Irish Government to just two categories. In short, the Irish taxpayer picked up the bill for the costs of the inquiry and any compensation but remained in ignorance of exactly who was to blame. It was a situation that would endure because of previous undertakings given to the Christian Brothers, including the promise that there would be no prosecutions even though the evidence of criminal acts was overwhelming.

It had been intended that there would be a policy of 'name and shame', but that was blocked by a legal challenge made by the Christian Brothers. The Brothers sought and received permission to deal with abusers anonymously. Thus, the report does not state whether all abusers were members of religious orders in charge of schools, or whether external parties were involved. Notwithstanding the straitjacket imposed on the Commission, the report had a profound impact in Ireland and beyond. But a sustained wailing and gnashing of teeth in the face of such sustained criminal behaviour is worthless unless at the end there is a measure of justice for the victims. Without that there would be little to show other than a pile of platitudes.

In the event 'no naming and shaming' was followed by the revelation of a further twisting of the knife. An 'indemnity deal' had been signed between two representatives of the Conference of Religious of Ireland (CORI), an umbrella group representing 138 religious congregations, on behalf of eighteen religious orders that had run the residential institutions, and the then Minister of Education, Michael Woods. It would not have been unreasonable to expect that many of those responsible for the acts condemned by the Commission would end up in court, then in prison. Instead, the deal that had been cut between the government and CORI not only ensured immunity and privacy, it went even further: the religious orders were also indemnified from any legal action, whereby any costs would now be met by the Irish taxpayer in return for a transfer of property and assets to the sum of €128 million. No representatives of the victims had been involved in any of these negotiations.

The sum of €128 million did not even cover the cost of the Commission, leaving nothing to compensate the victims. This deal remained secret until revealed by the news media in January 2003. It had been completed by a caretaker government at the time of the 2002 election, on the last possible day of business. As such the agreement had neither Cabinet approval nor the benefit of a debate on the issues within the Dáil. The overall cost to the Irish taxpayer has been put at €1 billion.

This currently is what passes for justice in Ireland for the victims of sexual and physical abuse. In June 2009, Pope Benedict yet again demonstrated that he inhabits a very rarefied area untouched by reality. Talking to the Irish bishops Martin and Brady, the Pope urged them:

'To establish the truth of what has happened, ensure that justice is done for all, put in place the measures that will prevent these abuses happening again, with a view to healing for survivors.'

This meeting between Benedict and the two bishops took place a month after the Ryan Report had been published. The Pope's appeal was directed not just at the two men sitting before him but to the entire Catholic Church of Ireland and to its priests and nuns. Quite simply, he was asking the Church to find a satisfactory solution. Many priests within that Church would appear to have concluded in the lights of the various clauses in the 'indemnity deal' that they already had a satisfactory solution.

This was not and is not a problem confined to the orphanages, schools of correction and institutions. In Ireland there were wider lessons to be learned. Even after the meticulous detail contained within the Ryan Report was published the apologists continued to deny the truth, doubtless motivated by a sentiment shared by many within the Vatican and other places 'for the good of Mother Church'. They hid behind a quiver of curious arguments: 'This was only a small minority of priests . . . These children who were allegedly abused, well nothing has been proved in court . . . They were all ne'er do wells, part of the criminal class . . . this survey only looked at children being held in residential institutions and industrial schools.' That last argument had particular resonance for the traditional Catholic. 'Take a survey of the Dublin

Archdiocese and you will get a quite different picture', went the argument. Sometimes life is well written.

Next up for consideration was the Murphy Report, again named after its Chairperson, Judge Yvonne Murphy, with the mandate to report on the handling by Church and State authorities of a representative sample of allegations and suspicions of child sexual abuse against clerics operating under the aegis of the Archdiocese of Dublin over the period 1975 to 2004.

Judge Murphy and her Commission were appointed in November 2005; their report was published in November 2009. Publication was delayed for some six months by the government, and was only eventually released because the Irish High Court ruled that it should be. At the eleventh hour, the Irish Government, who were of course fully aware of the report's contents, asked the Court to further delay publication. The Court declined the application.

The Murphy Commission was working to a much smaller compass than the Ryan Report. Its time-frame was confined to twenty-nine years, and the representative sample of cases investigated was confined to the activities of forty-six priests. The report's introduction couched in calm neutral language calmly reveals quite shocking facts.

'It is important in the Commission's view not to equate the number of complaints with the actual instances of child sexual abuse. While a significant number of priests against whom allegations were made admitted child sexual abuse, some denied it. Of those investigated by the Commission, one priest admitted to abusing over 100 children, while another accepted that he had abused on a fortnightly basis during the currency of his ministry which lasted for over 25 years [a minimum of 650 separate sexual acts of abuse on children]. The total number of documented complaints recorded against those two priests is just over seventy. In another case, there is only one complaint but the priest has admitted abusing at least six other children.'

Officials of the Archdiocese of Dublin conveyed to the Commission that the various cases that had come to light over the previous thirty-five years had left the Church, in common with the general public,

'taken by surprise by the volume of the revelations . . . Church authorities have repeatedly claimed to have been, prior to the late 1990s, on a "learning curve" in relation to the matter. Having completed its investigation, the Commission does not accept the truth of such claims and assertions.'

Yet again, the spectre of suppression of the truth for the good of Mother Church raises its head.

'The Dublin Archdiocese's pre-occupations in dealing with cases of child sexual abuse, at least until the mid 1990s, were the maintenance of secrecy, the avoidance of scandal, the protection of the reputation of the Church and the preservation of its assets. All other considerations, including the welfare of children and justice for victims, were subordinated to these priorities. The Archdiocese did not implement its own canon law rules and did its best to avoid any application of the law of the State.'

Not much comfort for the apologists is to be found in those conclusions. Indeed, as can be seen, although the area of investigations differed vastly from Justice Ryan's epic investigation of industrial schools and orphanages, the evidence and the conclusions to be drawn from the respective reports have an overwhelming symmetry. As for the 'learning curve' pleading of ignorance, Archbishop McQuaid was dealing with such cases in the 1950s and 1960s. There have been bishops all over the world who have used this defence during the past thirty years. Any adult male – be he a bishop or a man in any other walk of life – who did not know long before this scandal became public knowledge that grown men having sex with children is wrong and insidiously harmful to children is either an idiot or a liar or both.

Archbishop McQuaid and the three previous archbishops of Dublin during the period under investigation – Ryan, McNamara and Connell – do not emerge from this examination with any honour. The report observes:

'Not one of them reported his knowledge of child sexual abuse to the Gardaí throughout the 1960s, 1970s, or 1980s. It was not until November 1995 that Archbishop Connell allowed the names of seventeen priests about whom the Archdiocese had received complaints to be given to the Gardaí. This figure was not complete. At that time there was knowledge within the Archdiocese of at least twenty-eight priests against whom there had been complaints.'

Of the specific actions, or lack of them by the various Archbishops, the Commission comments:

'Archbishop McQuaid was familiar with the requirements of Canon law but did not apply them fully. It is clear that his dealings with Fr Edmondus in 1960 were aimed at the avoidance of scandal and showed no concern for the welfare of children.'

The name 'Edmondus' is a pseudonym. The priests cooperating with the Commission were given the option of
hiding behind a fictitious name. Thirty-three of the forty-
six took advantage of that offer.

> 'Archbishop Ryan failed to properly investigate com-
> plaints, among others, against Fr McNamee, Fr Mac-
> guire, Fr Ioannes, Fr Septimus and Fr Carney. He also
> ignored the advice given by a psychiatrist in the case of
> Father Moore that he should not be placed in a parish
> setting. Moore was subsequently convicted of a ser-
> ious sexual assault on a young teenager while working
> as a parish curate . . .
> 'Archbishop McNamara . . . restored priestly facul-
> ties to Fr Carney despite his having pleaded guilty to
> charges of child sexual abuse in 1983 and despite the
> fact that there were suspicions about him in relation to
> numerous other children. He failed to ensure that Fr
> Carney obeyed instruction and allowed him, in effect,
> to flout the wishes of his superiors.'

Tellingly, the snapshot of Archbishop McNamara finishes
with, 'He saw the need for insurance cover and started the
process of getting it.'

Of Archbishop Connell, the Commission remarks that

> '[He] saw very few of the complainants. (His prede-
> cessors do not appear to have seen any.) Of those he
> did see, some found him sympathetic and kind but
> with little understanding of the overall plight of vic-
> tims. Others found him remote and aloof.'

One area where Archbishop Connell demonstrated great
activity was with regard to the civil litigation against the
archdiocese. He personally approved the defences which

were filed by the archdiocese. Liability for injury or damage was never admitted. The Commission, commenting on this, observed, 'The Archbishop's strategies in the civil cases, while legally acceptable, often added to the hurt and grief of many complainants.'

As one moves further into the report the calmness of the carefully chosen words increases the power of the exposure that is unfolding: the turf wars between vying prelates, the arrogance of some, the apparent incomprehension of others, and above all the desire of the overwhelming majority of Church officers within Dublin to at all times hide, conceal and mask the truth is staggering. The buck-passing is of an Olympic standard. At regular intervals in the report the power of the understatement of particular facts shocks the reader.

The Commission found no direct evidence of a paedophile ring among the priests in the Dublin archdiocese, but there were 'some worrying connections'.

'Fr Carney and Fr McCarthy abused children during their visits to children's homes. They also brought children on holidays and shared accommodation with two separate complainants. A boy who was initially abused by Fr McCarthy was subsequently abused by Fr Carney. Fr Carney abused children at swimming pools and was sometimes accompanied to the swimming pools by Fr Macguire.

'When Fr Ioannes was being investigated for the abuse of a young boy, Father Boland, who was not a priest in the diocese at the time, turned up at the young boy's home offering comfort and took the opportunity to abuse the young boy himself.'

Within another part of the report (Chapter 11), the Commission explains the method used to select which priests to

interview. They had received information concerning complaints, suspicions or knowledge of child sexual abuse in
respect of 172 named priests and eleven unnamed priests.

> 'After a preliminary examination the Commission
> concluded that 102 of these priests were within remit.
> Of those priests who were not within the Commis-
> sion's terms of reference, two main reasons for their
> exclusion were identified:
> • the complaint was made outside the time period
> 1975–2004;
> • the priest was not operating under the aegis of
> the Archdiocese of Dublin at the time of the alleged
> abuse. The priests in question were mainly mem-
> bers of religious order and societies who were
> working in Dublin but not on behalf of the Arch-
> diocese.'

The criteria indicate the scruples that were applied. The
Commission then chose a representative sample from the
group of 102. Again the even-handed approached that was
applied, which is fully explained within the report, is
impressive. No one reading this report will ever be able
to claim that this is the work of a kangaroo court. The
implications of the very careful criteria applied lead the
reader irresistibly to the conclusion that what they found
with regard to the forty-six priests examined, they would
also have found existed within the remaining fifty-six
priests. It is a fact that should be borne in mind as one
considers just some fragments of two of the forty-six case
histories.

Marie Collins was one of a number of people abused by
Father Edmondus. She was severely affected by the abuse as
part of her statement to the Commission illustrates.

'Father [Edmondus] betrayed the trust invested in him by his religious superiors. He betrayed the trust of the hospital authorities. He betrayed my parents' trust. All had given me into his care. He betrayed my trust and my innocence. He abused his power and used my respect for his religious position to abuse and degrade me – a child – not just a child but a *sick child*. How much lower than that can you sink? *A man like that deserves our prayers not our protection* [emphasis in original].'

Father Edmondus committed a number of sexual assaults on young patients aged between eight and eleven in Our Lady's Hospital for Sick Children, Crumlin, in the late 1950s and 1960s. Sixteen years later he was based in County Wicklow, where he committed a sexual assault on a nine-year-old child. As the report notes, 'The case also falls to be considered by the Commission because, in the 1990s, suspicions about his behaviour while he was a curate in a North Dublin parish were brought to the attention of the Archdiocese.' Father Edmondus was born in 1931 and ordained in 1957. He subsequently held a number of appointments in the Dublin archdiocese.

In August 1960, the then head of the Catholic Church in Dublin, Archbishop McQuaid, was advised that a roll of camera film sent to a UK company for developing had been passed by a security officer to Scotland Yard who, having established that the owner was resident in Ireland, referred the matter to the commissioner of the Gardaí. There is no evidence of any subsequent investigation by the Irish police. The matter instead was handled in a manner very typical of the time. A quiet conversation between Police Commissioner Costigan and the archbishop took place. McQuaid was advised that the UK photographic company had 'handed to Scotland Yard a

colour film with label Rev. [Edmondus], Children's Hospital, Crumlin, Dublin, of which twenty-six transparencies
were of the private parts of two small girls aged ten or
eleven years.' The police commissioner asked the archbishop to take over the case because a priest was involved
and the Gardaí 'could prove nothing'. On the contrary,
the evidence was already in their hands.

Despite the fact that there was such irrefutable evidence
of sexual abuse, the police commissioner told the archbishop he would do nothing further, and nothing is exactly
what the Irish police did. As for the negatives and the film –
they vanished. McQuaid referred the matter to his auxiliary, Bishop Dunne, who expressed the view that a *crimen
pessium* – 'the worst crime', which includes child sexual
abuse – had been committed.

The following day Archbishop McQuaid met Father
Edmondus, who admitted photographing the children in
sexual postures alone and in groups. McQuaid made a note
of the meeting which in parts reads.

'The children were playing about, lifting their clothes.
He [Father Edmondus] rebuked them. Seeing this was
a chance of discovering what the genitals were like, he
pretended there was no film in the camera he was
carrying and photographed them in sexual postures,
alone and seated together, chiefly in a way or posture
that opened up the parts. He had declared that he had
done so, as one would take an art photo, seeing no
grave sin at all and suffering no physical disturbance in
himself. He was puzzled, though as he had seen line
drawings, as to structure and functions of female. In
questioning I discovered that he had been reared with
brothers, [in fact Edmondus also had a sister] had
never moved about socially with girls and tended to
avoid them as in the hospital with the nurses. I

suggested I get Doctor 'Rutherford' *a good Catholic to instruct him and thus end his wonderment . . .*

'I felt that he clearly understood the nature of the sinful act involved and to send him on retreat would defame him.'

Thus the Archbishop of Dublin displayed not only a dangerous level of naivety but a concern that was solely directed to the priest, not least in assisting him in his 'wonderment'. McQuaid made no effort to establish the identity of the young girls. Neither did he consider it appropriate to contact the Crumlin hospital or put protocols in place for future chaplains of the hospital. In view of the fact that the archbishop was the chairman of the board of directors, the omission of safeguards for the future was tantamount to an act of criminal negligence.

The archbishop conferred with Bishop Dunne and both men agreed that there was not an objective and subjective crime of the type envisaged in the 1922 instruction regarding *crimen pessium*, and consequently that there was no need to refer the matter to the Holy Office in Rome. One of the consequences of the archbishop's failure to take action was to place a ticking time bomb in the children's hospital, which remained unaware that it had been left in a highly vulnerable position. Father Edmondus saw Doctor Rutherford on three occasions. Any reports from the doctor had been removed from the Church files at the time the Commission was sitting.

The fact that the photographs had been taken by deception at a time when no nursing staff were present and that the film was sent to the UK for developing would indicate criminal intent to any normal observer. Clearly neither the archbishop nor his bishop came into that category. Bishop Dunne had demonstrated a remarkable flexibility in this thinking process. His initial conclusion was that a *crimen pessium* had definitely been committed. A mere three days and a further meeting with his archbishop had transformed his opinion completely.

The Commission concluded that the archbishop's motive was to avoid a scandal both in Ireland and in Rome. The current Archbishop of Dublin, Diarmuid Martin, accepts that his predecessor's conclusions were wrong, and that the measures taken were inadequate, but disturbingly he does not accept that McQuaid was motivated by a desire to avoid a scandal in both Ireland and Rome.

In many ways since these commissions in Ireland began, Diarmuid Martin has been at the forefront of change, standing resolute and condemning the old guard who are continuing to resist change, but in this issue it would seem that the archbishop still does not 'get it'. Marie Collins, one of the young girls abused at the Crumlin hospital in 1960 had attempted long before the Murphy Commission to get some acknowledgement of what had occurred and also an undertaking that Father Edmondus would be kept well away from children. In 1985 she talked to her local curate, Father Eddie Griffin. She was in the process of giving him a full account when the curate told her that he did not want to know the name of her abuser because then 'I would have to do something about it.' Subsequently explaining his position to the Irish police some nineteen years later in 2004 when the Commission was highly visible, he said:

> 'We as priests had been advised at college not to seek the name of priests that allegations were being made against. Marie Collins didn't tell me the name of the priest. I told her not to feel any guilt about what had happened and that the priest had done wrong and if she had guilt I could give her absolution.'

So, having instructed Mrs Collins not to give him the identity of her abuser he told the police, '. . . I wondered why she was there and thought she might be feeling guilty.' Indeed, many victims of clerical sexual abuse do feel guilt. They also feel deep shame. They also want steps taken to control the offending priest. What Father Griffin failed to grasp was that he had just been advised of a serious criminal offence. It was to be another ten long years before Marie was able to pluck up the courage and report the abuse to Archbishops House in 1995. The perpetrator of the crime meanwhile had continued to indulge his sexual desires.

In 1993, while Edmondus was a curate in Edenmore, North Dublin, his constant sexual grooming of young children eventually caused complaints to be made. Bishop Moriarty, the auxiliary priest for the area, discovered that Father Edmondus was in the habit of driving young children around, allowing them to change and put on their swimming costumes in his house; he would give them money and encouraged a group of youngsters who were perpetual truants to spend time with him. No adults were allowed into his house – he favoured instead the very young. The bishop discussed the problem with local priests and with Archbishop Connell, then contented himself with warning Father Edmondus about his behaviour and 'advising' him to refrain from the activities referred to above. No attempt was made by the archdiocesan authorities to check the archives or other files relating to Edmondus when these various complaints were received. Information was also acquired at this time that Edmondus was recording children's voices and, when questioned about this activity, he admitted also photographing children.

Apart from her attempt in 1985 to obtain help from her local curate – an experience which left Marie Collins even more traumatised than previously – this severely psycho-

logically damaged woman had suffered silently for nearly
thirty-five years. What had finally nerved her to try again
with regard to contacting the Catholic authorities was the
concern that other children might have been abused by
Father Edmondus. Consequently, as well as contacting the
archbishop, Marie also wrote to the Crumlin hospital. It is
impossible to adequately grasp the private hell in which this
woman had been living for so many years. Many a priest in
many a country over the period since the early 1980s
confronted with a case of clerical sexual abuse on a young
victim had taken a position that they 'will get over it in time
. . . put it behind you . . . get on with your life,' and other
unctuous platitudes inspired by a total ignorance of the
damage that has been done to an innocent child. Men who
have led a celibate life are perhaps not the best-qualified
counsellors in a case involving sexual abuse.

Contacting the archdiocese in 1995 acted as a spur for
Marie Collins, apart from the Crumlin hospital, letters
began to flow to other sections of the Catholic Church;
her local priest and Bishop Forristal were just two more
recipients. Archbishop Connell referred the case to Monsignor Stenson but made no attempt to acknowledge her
letter. Collins' local priest also failed to reply. It must have
seemed to the victim that her task in obtaining natural
justice was tantamount to single-handedly dragging the
Irish Church into the late twentieth century. Though Monsignor Stenson believed Marie he did not tell her that there
had been other incidents and other concerns regarding
Father Edmondus at Crumlin hospital. To have done so
would have given her not only psychological reassurance,
but encouragement that finally she was not fighting this
thing alone.

Neither was she told that she had directly led to a
significant breakthrough with regard to the Irish Church's
response to such cases. With the permission of Archbishop

Connell, the monsignor made a statement of partial disclosure to the police regarding Father Edmondus; this was a historic first. That it took until November 1995 for this to occur is unconscionable. Previously, many senior police officers, including police commissioners, regarded abusing priests as being outside their remit – thereby not only perpetuating such cases but creating a very attractive situation for would-be paedophiles.

When Monsignor Stenson outlined the nature of the abuse on Mrs Collins to the man responsible, Father Edmondus replied, 'I cannot place the girl,' but he accepted that 'inappropriate touching' could have happened. Later he observed, 'If I have a problem, it was with little girls.' He had, it transpired, no 'problem' with little boys.

Edmondus was referred for an assessment to the Grandana Institute in Shankill, Dublin. The institute is a service for those whose lives have been affected by sexual abuse, both victims and perpetrators. A December 1995 report on the priest recommended that he 'be removed from ministry as it is presently constituted'. The assessment was based on 'the escalatory nature of the alleged abuse . . . The alleged abusive pattern started with what appeared to be good natured innocent fun but was then followed by more sinister demands on the child.'

In March 1996, Mrs Collins met Monsignor Stenson again. She was anxious over several aspects and asked, 'Had Father Edmondus admitted the allegation that I made?' The monsignor confirmed that he indeed had. In fact he had not, he had merely agreed with the monsignor's suggestion. Stenson confirmed to Marie that Edmondus was not in the parish, was living in a religious house and was receiving therapy. In his written record of the meeting he observed that he was satisfied that 'she is not out to make difficulties for Father Edmondus or indeed the Church.' Yet again that theme of protecting Mother Church rears its head. No cover-up was too great; no deceit too large. Anything and everything had to be done to hide the truth and thus protect the reputation of the Roman Catholic Church, not from wicked lies, but from the unvarnished truth.

Contrary to what Marie Collins had been told, Father Edmondus was still living in the parish, despite being ordered to leave. He had also been left in his position by Cardinal Connell, who told him he was not to minister in the parish. Cardinal Connell told the Commission that the reason he had left the priest in place was 'because there had been nothing against [Edmondus] for something like thirty years, and it seemed to me a bit too harsh. *I did [it] in the interest of the children.*'

It was of course incorrect to say there had been nothing against this priest for thirty years, as a reading of his own files would have demonstrated to the cardinal. Despite the archbishop's instructions, Father Edmondus carried on exactly as before the instructions. Once he had left the community, he continued to visit the parish frequently, dressed in clerical attire and continued to hear confession. No one monitored his activities and he continued to be listed as a curate in Edenmore throughout 1996 and 1997.

The Gardaí, having been prodded by Marie Collins, finally decided to take a fresh look at her case. At a meeting with Monsignor Stenson they asked for a copy of the Father Edmondus file, or at least the opportunity to study it. Stenson's earlier groundbreaking activities with regard to giving the police some bare details on the priest had in the interim been reconsidered. He refused to give them a copy of the letter, stating he would need legal advice. He refused to let them read the file, declaring that Canon Law prevented such an action. He expressed dismay that Marie Collins had shown the police his letter to her in which he had written of Father Edmondus admitting the offence, he also refused to make a statement to that effect. Clearly the monsignor was not in the giving vein that day.

This entire affair was dogged – as so many abuse cases were and indeed still are – by far too many officials within the Catholic Church continually disregarding injunctions from the Vatican concerning transparency. Every archdiocese in the world continues to protect its secret files, continues to cover up what it deems is inappropriate to be aired.

It was only after an advisory panel made a number of basic recommendations regarding the Edmondus case that common sense began to prevail a little. Among those recommendations was 'the Archbishop should meet Marie Collins and offer a support person.' In December 1996 Archbishop Connell met Mrs Collins and her support priest Father James Norman. During this meeting the archbishop apologised to Marie for the 'hurt caused to her'. Father Norman kept a note of this meeting, and what follows is verbatim:

'During the meeting Marie raised a letter she had written to the Archbishop of the 4th of June [1996] concerning Edmondus' future. The Archbishop failed to give an explanation why he had not replied to her letter except to say it had raised very difficult questions.

'When Marie asked the Archbishop why he had not given a statement to the Gardaí confirming that there was another case on file from the 1960s the Archbishop replied that it would undermine people's confidence in the Church if they thought files were being passed to the Gardaí, i.e. annulment cases. He also said that the previous case was not serious as it only involved the taking of photographs.'

It would appear that the archbishop was at that moment ignorant of what there was within his own files on Edmondus. Father Norman's notes continue: 'Marie outlined in detail how having that type of photography taken had hurt and damaged her. The Archbishop was very shocked and upset by the story that Marie had told him.'

Subsequently, Marie asked the archbishop why he had not followed the framework document, a series of guidelines to assist bishops in correct procedure when dealing with abuse cases. His comment that it was 'not binding in canon or civil law, therefore, I could follow what parts I wanted to follow' was followed by the observation, 'I had to protect the good name of the priest who had abused you.'

In March 1997 Father Edmondus was arrested and charged with offences relating to the abuse of a child in County Wicklow parish and also the sexual abuse of Mrs Collins. In June 1997 Father Edmondus pleaded guilty to two counts of indecent assault of Marie Collins. Some days later he pleaded guilty to two counts of indecent assault on the girl in County Wicklow parish. He was sentenced to eighteen months' imprisonment in respect of the assaults on Mrs Collins and nine months' imprisonment to run concurrently in respect of the County Wicklow assaults. In November 1997 the total sentence was reduced on appeal to nine months. Prior to the case he had met Mrs Collins and he had apologised to her and offered to make a financial contribution to her.

Following the conviction a variety of people made statements. Archbishop Connell condemned child abuse as 'wrong and evil'. He also claimed that the dioceses had been cooperating with the Gardaí. When this was contested, Monsignor Stenson observed that the diocese never claimed it had cooperated fully, with emphasis on the word 'fully', with the Gardaí.

In May 1998, Father Edmondus was released from

prison; he was retired from active ministry under monitored conditions. The fact that this man was eventually brought to justice was entirely due to the efforts of the woman who had suffered sexual abuse as a young girl. Marie Collins triumphed despite the best efforts of the Gardaí, the Archdiocese of Dublin and a considerable number of bishops and priests.

Below are some quotes from the Commission's assessment of this case. Their full assessment can be read on pages 205 to 209 of their report:

'. . . Archbishop McQuaid's conclusion that Fr Edmondus' actions rose merely from a *"wonderment"* about the female anatomy is risible . . . Either Archbishop McQuaid could not deal with the fact that a priest who was in a privileged position of chaplain to a children's hospital fundamentally abused that position and sexually exploited vulnerable young children awaiting treatment or he needed an explanation which would deal with Bishop Dunne's justifiable concern and which would also justify not reporting the matter to Rome. The Commission considers that the second explanation is the more likely one.

'. . . How he [the local curate] could have formed the view that she might be feeling guilty and in need of absolution when, in fact, she was disclosing abuse is difficult for the Commission to understand.

'His assertion that, as priests, they had been advised in college not to seek the names of priests against who allegations were being made in a spiritual or counselling context is a cause for great concern to the Commission. Such an attitude would explain in large measure the many appalling deficiencies in the Church's handling of complaints of child sexual abuse over the years. Even if he himself did not wish to hear the full details of her complaint, he should have arranged for her to see his parish priest or another person who was in a position to deal with the complaint.'

'The Commission is particularly concerned that the Archdiocese seems to have been in breach of the guideline which states, "If the bishop or religious superior is satisfied that child sexual abuse has occurred, appropriate steps should be taken to ensure that the accused priest or religious does not remain in any pastoral appointment which affords access to children." The fact that Father Edmondus was allowed to wear clerical attire, attend at parish frequently and fulfil parish functions, despite having been allegedly removed from the parish by the Archbishop, was particularly worrying. Cardinal Connell told the Commission that it was not his fault that Father Edmondus did not obey instructions. Unfortunately this comment again underlines the failure of the Archdiocese to properly monitor priests who are disciplined.

'Everything that Mrs Collins managed to extract from the Archdiocese over the years . . . was given grudgingly and always after a struggle . . . there is no doubt that Mrs Collins, in her brave and often lonely campaign . . . was instrumental in changing the Archdiocese's understanding of these cases and of bringing about a far greater atmosphere of openness about the incidence and handling of child sexual abuse.'

In June 1992 Father Noel Reynolds was appointed parish priest of Glendalough in County Wicklow. He was at this time approaching his sixtieth birthday and had been a priest for just over thirty years. This was his first such appointment. His earlier career included periods as a chaplain at a number of girls' schools, before being appointed as curate to Kilmore Road parish in 1969. He was at this stage already sexually abusing children. His approach varied. Years later, one of the mothers who gave evidence to the Commission recounted how he had been a constant presence in her home over a seven-year period. 'He would take meals with the family and watch television with them. He would ask permission to wish the girls goodnight and unknown to her he was abusing them in their bedroom.' His friendships with children were widely noted in the parish. He constantly brought young children to his home, he also organised outings to the seaside. He would later admit abusing children in all of the many locations where he was posted.

A fellow priest walking into Father Reynolds' bedroom to switch the lights off was shocked to see what he later estimated to be a woman of some thirty years of age asleep in Father Reynolds' bed. It seems unlikely to have been a thirty-year-old woman. Later during police interviews Reynolds admitted abusing a teenager over a period of two days at the time in question.

In 1983 he asked for a transfer from Dublin to an island posting so that he could 'be more in tune with the people'. He told the archbishop he wanted to 'separate myself from life in Dublin where there are far too many distractions'. He got his wish. No assessments were carried out and he was posted to the island of Tuam. Clearly the distractions came with him, as he later admitted to the police that he had abused a number of unidentified victims while on Tuam. A spell in Bonnybrook parish was followed by another as a curate in Saggart, County Dublin, before his appointment in Glendalough.

In 1995, some three years after he had taken up his duties, Archbishop Connell initiated a preliminary investigation of a number of complaints emanating from Glendalough. Monsignor Stenson was appointed as delegate, a form of clerical police superintendent. It took nearly five months to pin down the school principal and obtain an appointment. When that meeting eventually took place, the principal claimed that there had not been any physical or sexual abuse. He said that a parent had spoken directly to Father Reynolds about the matter and that the priest had indicated that it would stop. Those two statements are, of course, directly contradictory. The principal in his statement said.

> 'There was gossip and innuendo – I never left him in a class on his own subsequently. I didn't allow my daughter to be an altar girl. They were saying that he was talking about "making love" when the girls first spoke to me.'

Another parent had talked to the police about rumours the previous year that Father Reynolds was interfering sexually with local children. Monsignor Stenson interviewed Reynolds in March 1996. Reynolds admitted 'talking dirty' to the girls: '. . . jokes that you'd be embarrassed to tell in the company of their parents. Word games – a rhyme with sexy connotations.' But since the complaining parent had talked to him he had for the past two years 'stopped all this'. Reynolds continued to Monsignor Stenson:

> 'It was my own folly rather than maliciousness. I didn't want to frighten anyone or make them feel unsafe.
>
> 'Something similar had occurred in other parishes but never became public.
>
> 'If I had been assessed before going to Clonliffe [the Catholic diocesan seminary] I would have been considered a repressed person in need of affection. My mother died at four. Longing for love.

'In 1959 in Dundrum Tech I freaked giving children a class on sex education. I was always trying to disassociate the idea of dirt from sex . . .

'I believe loneliness as a child has been a huge factor. I would admit that my sexual orientation is towards children. Children would arouse me sexually . . .

'At sixty-three my judgement in these areas of children has been foolish. I think I can control it. It was a habit. I think I can avoid bad behaviour anymore – imprudent – folly. I will go for any help that is required.'

Shortly after this meeting, Father Reynolds expressed a desire to move to Moone (Moone County Kildare is the headquarters of the Cistercian Order). This seemed acceptable to Archbishop Connell, who was less than frank with the Abbot of Moone. What followed had an inevitability about it. Father Reynolds had a meeting with the abbot, who learned enough to cause his mental alarm bell to ring, at least softly. He wrote to Monsignor Stenson.

'In the course of our conversation he [Father Reynolds] told me about some incidents involving children while he was administering as P.P. [parish priest] at Glendalough. He had discussed the incidents with the Archbishop who told him to ask me to contact you. He seemed rather reticent about the whole matter and I didn't like to press him because it is a very sensitive area. But it would seem that there was a complaint made to Archbishops House. I would be glad, therefore, if you could let me know what you think I should know about these incidents.'

In May 1996, the abbot and the monsignor met. It was agreed that Father Reynolds should be assessed by someone such as Dr Patrick Walsh, with a view to assisting the monks and Father Reynolds to reach a decision. Reynolds did not join the Cistercians.

In March 1997, the case was referred to an advisory panel. Monsignor Stenson, as the delegate, produced a report for the panel. A month later, the panel concluded that it did not consider there was any firm evidence that any incidents of child sexual abuse had taken place, although it seemed clear that some inappropriate behaviour did happen.

Two years had elapsed since the decree issued by Archbishop Connell initiating a 'preliminary' investigation into the complaints about Father Reynolds and he still had the run of his parish. Now there was to be further evaluation, this time at the Granada Institute.

In May 1997, Dr Walsh issued a preliminary report. He noted that he could not give a definite conclusion 'until he had completed a more detailed assessment of Fr Reynolds's personality and the history of the problem'. Dr Walsh stated that Reynolds was capable of maintaining a positive and appropriate ministry to adults. In the doctor's opinion, Reynolds was capable of a positive and appropriate ministry to children but in a limited way.

'He recommended that Fr Reynolds should not be involved in non-structured or informal interactions with children in the parish or in school. He also recommended that Fr Reynolds should confine himself to the administration of the sacraments in the normal way but with the proviso that, when he heard confessions, he maintain the proper protocol and avoid physical contact and remain focused on the administration of the sacrament . . . he should not be involved in matters dealing with sexuality. Overall, Dr Walsh concluded that Father Reynolds had shown "considerable confu-

sion in his relationships with children. He has
confused his own needs as a child with their needs
and consequently has failed to maintain appropriate adult–child boundaries. In addition he has used
inappropriate language in his classes and interac-
tion with children.'

The doctor also recommended that a priest support person
be put in place for Reynolds. This was not done for over a
year. In the interim a course of action was decided upon by
Archbishop Connell that, like so much in the history of
clerical sexual abuse, was beyond belief. Less than two
months after the doctor's recommendations regarding future contact with children, the archbishop appointed Father
Reynolds to the National Rehabilitation Hospital in Dun
Laoghaire. The hospital caters not only for adults in need of
rehabilitation; it also has a children's ward and a school.
During the period that Reynolds was at the hospital there
were 646 in-patients, of whom ninety-four were aged
eighteen or younger.

The hospital was not informed of Reynolds' history. The
Granada Institute where he was still a patient was
not advised of the appointment. Neither was Bishop
O'Mahony, who as liaison bishop for hospital chaplains
should have been fully briefed. Indeed it was not until the
bishop was called to the hospital in May 1998 because of
concerns about Father Reynolds' physical health that he
became aware that the priest 'might have a problem with
child abuse'.

Bishop O'Mahony met with both Father Reynolds and
his specialist, Dr Walsh, in May 1998. Subsequently Dr
Walsh wrote to the bishop, declaring he was of the firm
view that Father Reynolds posed no threat to children but
he stressed that his recommendation referred to earlier,
regarding the parameters that should apply with regard

to any contact Father Reynolds had with children, should be adhered to.

By now the net was closing around Father Reynolds. A few months earlier, in February, the mother of one of his alleged victims spoke to Monsignor Dolan, indicating that her daughter had been sexually abused by a priest some twenty years earlier. She did not identify the priest; nor, surprisingly, was she asked to. She was also advised that as her daughter was now an adult she would have to make the complaint herself. The mother told the monsignor that she herself was having counselling because of the sexual abuse of her daughter. The Commission was later to observe that it found it strange that the identity of the assailant had not been asked for. The name would have led to the Reynolds file and the various admissions already on record.

Through all of this Father Reynolds continued to act as chaplain at the hospital. Six days after Dr Walsh wrote to O'Mahony reassuring him that his patient was harmless with regard to children, Monsignor Dolan was contacted by a social worker working at a drug treatment centre. One of her clients was alleging that she had been abused by Father Reynolds when she was nine years old.

In July 1998 Archbishop Connell finally released Father Reynolds from his duties as hospital chaplain. In November 1998 the mother who had initially contacted the archdiocese in February alleging that one of her daughters had been sexually abused returned. She identified the priest as Father Reynolds and now claimed that not one but two of her daughters had been sexually abused by him. Subsequently, she met with Father Reynolds and his support priest. At this meeting Reynolds acknowledged that he had indeed abused her two daughters.

Despite the fact that Reynolds had in front of witnesses freely admitted sexually abusing two young girls, the archdiocese still refused to report the matter to the police. They held the view that as the two sisters had shrunk from that ordeal it was not appropriate for the archdiocese to inform the police.

In June 1999 the police were advised of other complaints regarding Father Reynolds; these concerned sexual abuse while he was attached to the parish of Kilmore West in the late 1970s. It was clear by now from the statements in the possession of the police that the allegations were 'extremely serious'. The social worker at the drugs centre said it was the worst case of 'serious and systematic abuse' that she had ever encountered. By August 1999 there were starting to be some leaks to the newspapers. One report talked of rape by an elderly priest on two sisters. The paper also alleged that the priest had used a crucifix in what was described as a sick sex assault.

Father Reynolds had in January 1999 been found a place in a nursing home. He had been medically examined. There was cardiac disease, the initial stages of diabetes and Parkinson's disease. He was, however, well enough in August 1999 to travel to Rome to celebrate the fortieth anniversary of his ordination.

In October 1999, there was yet another complaint of sexual abuse; this was again in Kilmore West in the 1970s. This woman alleged that as she was preparing for her communion, Father Reynolds sat her on his knee and put his hands into her pants and put his fingers into her vagina. It was alleged that this had happened on five separate occasions prior to her first communion.

Father Reynolds was arrested in October 1999 for the offence of raping one of the two sisters referred to earlier, between the years 1971 and 1979. The police carried out a very thorough investigation into this case, and had extensive interviews with the accused priest. He admitted widespread abuse, including assaulting one of the sisters when she was eleven and the other when she was six years old, and putting his finger into their vaginas when they were in bed in their own home. He admitted inserting a crucifix into one girl's vagina and rectum. He said he had acknowledged to the girls' mother that he had abused her daughters and offered her £30,000 compensation, which she had declined. He offered in evidence to the police the crucifix he had used to abuse one of the sisters.

He told the police that he was sexually attracted to young girls and that they were not the only two victims in Kilmore. He could remember about twenty girls in total; there were others in East Wall and on the island of Tuam.

The police became aware of another twelve complainants. Nine made statements; the other three refused to do so. The incidents ranged from fondling of genitals to touching their legs, digital penetration, anal rape, attempted sexual intercourse and inviting children to fondle his penis. In total, nine females and six males claimed they had been abused by Father Reynolds. At the time of the various abuses they were aged between six and eleven. As the Commission observed within their report, 'Of course, he has admitted to many more cases of abuse, at least twenty in Kilmore alone.'

A very comprehensive file was forwarded by the police to the Director of Public Prosecutions (DPP), who had begun to process a prosecution when representations by the priest's solicitor concerning his client's declining health – specifically medically verified reports regarding the onset of dementia – persuaded the DPP to change his mind. It was a decision that left the two sisters, among others, 'bitterly disappointed with the outcome'.

The Commission outlined in detail the shocking behaviour of the archdiocese, beginning with its failure to take the correct course of action as early as 1994 – a failure that continued through the entire affair – is summarised in the Commission's assessment with a classic example of understatement: 'This case was extremely badly handled by the Archdiocese.' The various observations concluded with another dry observation: 'It seems to the Commission that a somewhat extraordinary approach was adopted towards Fr Reynolds.'

Between those two statements the Commission clinically dissects the case of Father Reynolds.

'. . . Numerous indications of serious abuse and of admissions by Fr Reynolds were ignored. The suspicions about Fr Reynolds surfaced during his time in Glenda-lough in 1994. Despite the fact that the parents had no desire to go to the Gardaí or to the health board, and wished the Church to deal with the matter, it was March 1996 before any interview with Fr Reynolds was con-ducted. He admitted to the complaints. He stated that something similar had happened in other parishes . . . Despite this admission he was allowed to remain on as parish priest in Glendalough until July 1997. The Com-mission accepts that Monsignor Stenson only became aware of the complaints in October 1995.

'In the interview with Monsignor Stenson in March 1996, Father Reynolds also admitted that his sexual orientation was towards children. A record of this inter-view is signed by Fr Reynolds. Again, despite this, he was given an appointment in the National Rehabilitation Hospital. This appointment gave him access to young children. Subsequently, Bishop O'Mahony became aware that Fr Reynolds may have a problem with child sexual abuse but he does not seem to have mentioned this to anyone else in the Archdiocese or, indeed, to the hospital. This, the Commission believes, represents a major breakdown in communications among those in overall charge in the Archdiocese'

The Commission concludes:

> 'It seems to the Commission that, had the two women themselves not complained to the Gardaí, the Archdiocese would have been quite happy to ignore the fact that any abuse had taken place.'

The Murphy Commission's overall conclusion to its entire investigation deserves to be read aloud from the pulpits of every Catholic Church, not only in Ireland but every Catholic Church throughout the world on a regular basis:

> 'The Commission has no doubt that the clerical child sexual abuse was covered up by the Archdiocese of Dublin and other Church authorities over much of the period covered by the Commission's remit. The structures and rules of the Catholic Church facilitated that cover up. The State authorities facilitated the cover up by not fulfilling their responsibilities to ensure that the law was applied equally to all and allowing the Church institutions to be beyond the reach of the normal law enforcement processes. The welfare of the children, which should have been the first priority, was not even a factor to be considered in the early stages. Instead the focus was on the avoidance of scandal and the preservation of the good name, status and assets of the institution and of what the institution regarded as its most important members – the priests. In the mid 1990s a light began to be shone on the scandal and the cover up. Gradually, the story has unfolded. It is the responsibility of the State to ensure that no similar institutional immunity is ever allowed to occur again. This can be ensured only if all institutions are open to scrutiny and not accorded an exempted status by any organs of the State.'

There was a wide consensus on the facts that the Murphy Commission had established and to their conclusions. What had been exposed yet again was the fallaciousness of Pope John Paul II when he had observed that clerical sexual abuse of children was 'an American problem'. Many within the Vatican at the time of this utterance wholeheartedly agreed with the Holy Father. Many today, not only within the Vatican but much further afield, still cling to other myths that surround the issue. They dismiss any evidence that contradicts the views they hold and the opinions they glibly express.

Within a month of the report's publication in November 2009, four bishops had resigned. They stepped down under heavy pressure from public opinion, media condemnation and the clear prompting of Dublin's archbishop, Diarmuid Martin.

The archbishop had by November 2009 got up a power-ful head of steam. Apart from cutting a swathe through the bishops of Ireland, he had gone after the eighteen religious orders who, as a result of a much earlier investigation of clerical sexual abuse known as the Hussey Commission, had agreed to provide some €128 million in compensation to victims of child abuse. The money was to be raised through a combination of transfers of cash, property and land. It was a very cosy settlement for the religious orders, with clauses that stipulated that any victims who accepted monetary settlements would waive the right to sue either Church or government. Furthermore, the identities of the abusing priests were to be kept secret.

Despite the fact that they had squeezed such terms from the victims, seven years later, Archbishop Martin discovered that very typically they had failed to honour the terms of payment. It was a failure that the archbishop described as 'stunning'. Before he had finished with them most of the religious orders were equally stunned. Martin's efforts on behalf of the victims included personally delivering to the Pope a letter from the representatives for abuse victims asking for €1 billion in compensation. The total compensation paid was approximately €1.2 billion. The originally promised €128 million had become a mere 10 per cent of the final total.

The Christian Brothers also felt the heat from the redoubtable archbishop. Their reputations had been largely destroyed by the Ryan Report, yet they too had cavilled about what could be regarded as proper compensation. Eventually in late November 2009 they offered a $242 million package to settle the claims of the surviving people who had been abused as children by the Christian Brothers. They also expressed the Order's 'shame and sorrow' for the abuse uncovered by the Ryan Commission. One of the outgoing prelates, Bishop James Moriarty, denied that he had ignored complaints of sexual abuse but conceded, 'I should have challenged the prevailing culture.'

Meanwhile, Pope Benedict's response to the continuing long Lent in Ireland was a declaration that he shared the 'outrage, betrayal and shame' felt by the Irish people over the Murphy Report. The Pope was 'disturbed and distressed' by the contents of the report. Pope Benedict also promised a pastoral letter.

There were plenty of other countries in need of comfort and guidance, including the United States. The US bishops' annual report for 2009 revealed a continuing rise in the figure the clerical abuse scandal was costing the US Catholic Church. Yet again the figures were incomplete: five eparchies and the Diocese of Lincoln refused to supply any figures for the audit. The overall cost, again including settlements, therapy for victims, attorneys' fees, support for offenders and other expenses was a figure close to $230 million.

The report found that 398 new credible allegations were lodged against 286 diocesan priests or deacons in 2009. Behind the cold impersonal figures are some very disturbing stories. In July 2009 the Archdiocese of Chicago paid out $4 million to settle six abuse cases. The cases involved sexual abuse by four priests between 1970 and 1986; the evidence that had emerged included a glimpse of how the prolonged cover-up by the diocese functioned. Bishop Raymond Goedert's 180-page deposition was a powerful condemnation of the corruption that had abounded within the archdiocese:

'I knew that the civil law considered sexual abuse a crime but Church law required me to treat such matters confidentially. I simply would not talk about the cases to anyone except those who had a right to know within the Diocese.'

The Church believed, and in many quarters continues to believe, that it functions on a higher plane than man-made laws, although of course Church law is also man-made.

Marc Pearlman one of the attorneys representing the victims observed:

'What emerges here is that the interests of the institution come first then the man, the perpetrator of the crime. And somewhere in the distance are the victims of the crime.'

Between June 2001 and June 2008 the Chicago Archdiocese paid out $80.2 million in legal settlements relating to clerical sexual abuse. Yet again, evidence confirmed that the global secret system had operated in the archdiocese for decades. Thus serial predators were moved from parish to parish, contaminating more and more victims. They were protected by a deeply ingrained institutional secrecy 'for the good of Mother Church's name'. Bishop Goedert's deposition admitted that he knew that at least twenty-five priests had sexually abused children but he had not reported them.

In September 2009 a very similar story unfolded on the west coast. The cover-up had been ordered by Cardinal Roger Mahony of the Los Angeles Archdiocese, who instructed a subordinate to delay reporting clerical sexual abuse to the police until the priest in question could be defrocked. The priest, the Reverend Michael Baker, was eventually defrocked in December 2000; the archdiocese did not report the abuse claims against Baker to the police until 2002. At that time Baker was charged with thirty-four counts of sexual abuse involving six victims. He had originally told Mahony in 1986 that he had molested two boys from 1978 to 1985. Instead of immediately advising the police, Mahony sent the priest to a residential facility that treated sexually abusing priests. Baker was subsequently assigned to nine different parishes but barred from having one-to-one contact with minors, a restriction he violated at least three times. After Baker was finally charged under a Californian law that allowed the prosecution of cases involving acts before 1988 the US Supreme Court voided the Californian law. Again the unwritten law 'protect the abusing priest' had prevailed.

Vermont also offered examples of the application of the unwritten law. In October 2009 a Vermont court awarded $2.2 million to a sexual-abuse victim for negligence by the Burlington Diocese in their supervision of the abuser, Father Edward Paquette. The diocese had previously been ordered to pay $12 million to other victims of Father Paquette and a further twenty cases were pending.

This desire to protect the guilty, to resist every conceivable attempt made on behalf of victims of clerical sexual abuse continued to demonstrate the total contempt displayed by many dioceses to papal injunctions on the issue of greater transparency. In November 2009 the Diocese of Bridgeport, Connecticut, having lost an entire series of legal battles in its attempts to prevent the disclosure of files relating to the handling of sexual abuse complaints, filed yet another motion with a Connecticut court asking a judge to reconsider his order for release of diocesan documents. The diocesan lawyers filed documents acknowledging that eight priests in one parish had been accused of sexual abuse over a period of years, but argued that there is no need to release further documentation. The Bridgeport Diocese had previously failed in every effort it had made to overturn a State Court order, including appeals to the Connecticut Supreme Court and the US Supreme Court.

The Diocese of Fairbanks, which stretches across the most northerly two thirds of Alaska but has fewer than 15,000 Catholics, a mere forty-six parishes and just twenty-one priests, had filed for bankruptcy in the previous year, reaching an agreement in November 2009 to settle the claims of nearly 300 abuse victims for $10 million. That somewhere so remote and removed from the mainstream United States should have suffered such sexual abuse of children powerfully demonstrates that this particular plague reaches to the furthest corners.

By 2010 the concern within the Roman Catholic hierarchy in the United States regarding the continuing financial fall-out caused by the large compensation awards in the clerical sexual abuse cases had deepened dramatically. Though the number of fresh cases of abuse had dropped very considerably since the high figures recorded at the beginning of the decade, it was the abuses that had occurred in earlier years that seemed to be without end. Though the US Church remained the wealthiest in the world, the continuing substantial settlements during a period of recession left a number of dioceses between a rock and a hard place.

At least seven had filed for bankruptcy in the recent past. Others resorted to selling real estate to pay the victims.

In Connecticut during March 2010 a draft bill calling for an extension on the statutes of limitations in child sexual abuse cases posed a particular acute moral dilemma. On 10 and 11 April 2010 a letter created by the bishops of the state was read out at every mass:

> 'Connecticut already has the longest retroactive statute in the United States – thirty years past the age of eighteen . . . House Bill 5473 would make Connecticut the only State without a statute of limitations. The bill would put all Church institutions, including your parish at risk.'

Their letter was not without hyperbole:

> 'Claims could be made . . . that might be fifty, sixty, seventy years old or older. More often, these claims would be difficult to defend because key individuals are deceased, memories have faded and documents and other evidence have been lost.'

The likelihood of a victim in his or her nineties mounting the witness box would seem improbable. Each case would surely be considered on its merits. In the event the bill was withdrawn, having failed to attract sufficient support in House and State Senate. Anyone mounting a claim in Connecticut in their forty-ninth year, thirty years after their eighteenth birthday when they can first make an accusation, is thus doomed to failure. In many other states the retroactive period is considerably shorter. The bill's defeat was acclaimed by a spokesman for the bishops, not least because some sixty sexual abuse cases against the St Francis Hospital and the late Dr George Reardon who had worked at the hospital from 1963 to 1993 would not now be able to proceed. The victims had been denied their day in court. Previously, when Reardon died in 1998, those many victims had assumed that any chance of obtaining justice had died with him. However, in 2007, when the new owner was renovating the late doctor's house a cache of more than 50,000 slides and 100 reels of child pornography was discovered.

Concern about evidence relating to child abuse was not confined to the east coast: over in Los Angeles the arch-diocese was running very true to form three years after it had agreed to the largest priest abuse settlement in US history. A key element of that agreement – the public release of the personal files of the offending priest – had still not become a reality. The documents were viewed by the victims as a series of smoking guns that held yet to be revealed and important details of abuses that had already caused the diocese to part with $660 million. The victims lacked the resources to push the archdiocese to comply. Before the 2007 settlement, the diocesan offices had been awash with attorneys who smelled a modern-day Klondike. Once they had collected their large fees the circus had moved on.

For the many hundreds of victims it was an additional abuse, this time of their legal rights. On 26 May, 4,000 Catholics, including seven cardinals, fifty-nine bishops and 411 priests, welcomed Archbishop José Gomez as coadjutor archbishop of the United States' largest diocese at a Mass of Reception. 'As I near the end of my time of tending this corner of the Vineyard, the shepherd's staff is passed to Archbishop Gomez,' said Cardinal Roger Mahony. 'Mahony goes; Gomez comes. Christ alone endures.' As do the victims of the widespread clerical sexual abuse, waiting for vindication.

The dubious behaviour of another prince of the Church

was revealed during the same month that Cardinal Mahony was bidding goodbye to Los Angeles: Cardinal William Levada. In view of the fact that Levada was the current Pope's successor as head of the Congregation of the Faith (CDF), this was yet another indication of just how deeply the abuse scandal has penetrated the ranks of the prelates. It was established that while serving in two earlier positions as archbishop of Portland and subsequently archbishop of San Francisco, Levada had permitted at least four priests whom he knew had sexually abused children to remain in public ministry. Bearing in mind that the head of the CDF is responsible for the Catholic Church's response to clerical sexual abuse of children the implications of Levada's history are far reaching.

Erin Olson, a Portland lawyer who has been involved in numerous sexual abuse lawsuits against the Portland Archdiocese said,

> 'It's no surprise that the Catholic Church continues to be mired in the abuse scandal when the Cardinal in charge of how the Church as a whole responds to child sex abuse allegations, did such a poor job himself as bishop and archbishop.'

Contacted ten days before the *New York Times* published a long and detailed story on various aspects of his career, Cardinal Levada replied by email, stating that he did not have 'the time nor the access to records' to respond to the list of questions submitted to him. Instead he pointed the reporter to a homily he delivered at an apology ceremony for clerical-abuse victims in 2003, which the cardinal said might be helpful in 'understanding changes in my own thinking and behaviour as well as the evolution in approach taken by US Catholic bishops'.

The cardinal's own thinking and behaviour are recorded

earlier within this book. In 1985 Levada had met with the three men responsible for the manual for handling child sexual abuse cases, a document that – if acted upon by the US Church – would have saved not only much money but a great deal of suffering. Father Doyle and his two fellow authors spent a day going through the body of evidence and the conclusion of their report with Levada. The archbishop, as he then was, expressed great enthusiasm for all of the recommendations. At that moment he 'got it'. Some two weeks later he had lost it. The bishops, Levada reported, had shelved the report and would convene their own committee to examine the issue. There was in fact no committee; there was in fact no alternative plan.

Two decades later, when deposing evidence in the Portland sexual abuse scandals, Levada could recall little from his meeting with the three authors. The cardinal undoubtedly has his supporters who have rallied around the man who has pleaded a familiar defence within the homily referred to above, delivered in 2003. Levada talked of the importance of reporting incidents to authorities and removing 'priest offenders' from ministry.

> 'The whole Church has been shocked and scandalized by the abuse done by a *few* of her priests to children and young people . . . the Church is *slowly learning* how deep this wound is, how slow to heal and how diligent must be our effort to ensure that it will not happen again.' [author's italics]

His record at Portland and San Francisco shows a man 'who knew best', even when it was abundantly clear that he did not. Confronted with evidence that the Reverend Aldo Orso-Manzonetta had invited a boy to stay overnight at the rectory, Levada merely told the priest not to repeat the mistake. This was three years after Levada had had his all-day meeting with Father Doyle and his colleagues, during which the problem of serial abuse was one of the main topics discussed. Orso-Manzonetta did not respond to the gentle strictures Levada had uttered in 1988. Rumours continued to abound. In May 1992 the Reverend Charles Lienert, the archdiocese's vicar for clergy wrote to Levada, detailing the extensive history of accusations against Orso-Manzonetta. It was a further two years before yet another complaint by one of Orso-Manzonetta's victims prompted a psychological evaluation. A letter to the examining doctor from Lienert expressed concern about the 'sheer number of allegations . . . These records are discoverable should someone choose to sue us.' Orso-Manzonetta subsequently retired. He died in 1996.

The naivety that is implicit in much of Levada's response to clerical sexual abuse was on show from another quarter during May 2010. The Reverend Blase Cupich is chairman of the Committee for Children and Youth Protection of the US Conference of Catholic Bishops. In the *America* magazine he wrote an article headed 'Twelve Things the Bishops Have Learned from the Abuse Crisis'. The first of his 'twelve things' suffices to give a feel for his revelations.

> '1. The injury to victims is deeper than non-victims can imagine. Sexual abuse of minors is crushing precisely because it comes at a stage in their lives when they are vulnerable, tender with enthusiasm, hopeful for the future and eager for friendships based on trust and loyalty.'

The state of Connecticut has, it would seem, drawn a line in the sand and is going to take a militant position on as many issues as possible. Having won a resounding victory over attempts to rewrite the statute of limitations in April, in

May diocesan lawyers were back in the court again as an unidentified woman sought access to 661 pages of documents, including a 2005 letter about her alleged abuser, the Reverend Thomas Shea. The letter had been sent by the diocese to the then Cardinal Joseph Ratzinger. The woman claimed that she was a twelve-year-old parishioner when she was sexually assaulted by Shea and that the assault took place in St Joseph's Church. Her lawyer, Robert Reardon, is seeing reports, notes and letters about Shea from Church officials, the doctors and psychiatrists who treated him, and the parishioners who complained about him. He is also pressing for the release of the letter sent to Ratzinger. The diocese claims that the 661 pages are 'privileged communications not subject to disclosure'.

Reardon is convinced that the documents will show not only that Father Shea sexually abused his client but that the diocese and St Joseph's Church engaged in a conspiracy to protect sexually abusive priests by applying the secret system. The lawyer has complained that the documents that the diocese has already release portray Shea in a favourable light, even though he had a long record much of which was anything but 'favourable'.

Father Shea, now deceased, had a disturbing history during which he had been accused of molesting at least sixteen girls in eleven parishes within the diocese. Bishops frequently moved him from one church to another after parents complained about his behaviour, which often involved kissing and fondling young girls. The bishops never reported him to the police, yet when Bishop Daniel Reilly transferred Shea to St Joseph's Church in 1976 it was with orders that the priest be kept away from children in the parish school. In a 2004 interview with a Connecticut newspaper Father Shea denied fondling girls but in a curiously phrased observation he said:

'I would show what I considered a reasonable affection by whatever norms I had to work with, I would
just give them a simple kiss. There are things I wish I
hadn't done. *The fact is that there are some of these
things that they ought to have taught us in the seminary but didn't teach us.*' [author's italics]

One can but wonder exactly what kind of screening procedure, if any, was used on Shea before he was accepted as a
novice, and also what kind of regular monitoring was
applied. As of this time of writing the application by Robert
Reardon has yet to be resolved.

Amid the US court battles to establish truth and the
further revelations of abuse comes news of the continuing
price being paid by dioceses for crimes committed long ago.
As recorded earlier, in October 2009, the Burlington Diocese in Vermont was ordered to pay $2.2 million to a victim
of clerical abuse. In May 2010 the same diocese agreed to
pay over $20 million to settle twenty-nine lawsuits alleging
sexual abuse of minors, and at least a further $2.35 million
to three victims who had won jury trials.

In a letter of 13 May 2010 Bishop Salvatore Mantano of
Burlington wrote,

'I once again apologize most sincerely for the pain the
victims have suffered. I ask that you join me in praying
always for these wounded and hurt brothers and sisters
. . . I also beg our Lord's forgiveness for any insensitivity
or lack of charity which I may have shown throughout
this process.'

Just two weeks later came another act in this sad story. The
Catholic Church of Vermont agreed to sell its historic
thirty-two-acre headquarters overlooking Lake Champlain
to the alternative liberal arts college, Burlington College.

They have also advertised for sale the 26.5-acre Camp Holy Cross. The two sites will fetch at least $20 million. The abuse victims will get their respective payments and Vermont's Catholics will have lost an important part of their history.

In Boston the archdiocese is facing heavy tax payments for property in parishes that have been formally closed. Church properties are ordinarily exempt from taxation, but local officials confronted with budget pressures of their own are passing the pain on. They argue that if the buildings are not being used for religious purpose then they are taxable.

In Delaware a bankruptcy judge has recently ruled that creditors in the Catholic Diocese of Wilmington can try to lay claim to assets of certain parishes held by the diocese. The ruling means that the alleged victims of sexual abuse by priests can pursue the entire $120 million in the pooled account. It is an account that contains not only the diocesan funds of $45 million but also funds held in trust by the diocese on behalf of various parishes; a hornet's nest in the making, as it places the whole archdiocese under the threat of bankruptcy.

If the late Father Shea felt there were 'things they ought to have taught us', one wonders how he would have responded to the kind of questioning and screening that awaits a man who in today's world believes he has a vocation for the priesthood.

'When was the last time you had sex?' is one of the first questions asked of a candidate. The preferred answer should be at least 'three years ago'. 'What kind of sexual experiences have you had? Do you like pornography?' He will be asked those questions, and a great deal more in a similar vein, including a compulsory HIV test and a 587-question questionnaire – the Minnesota Multiphasic Personality Inventory, which screens for depression, paranoia and gender confusion. Exactly how effective these various techniques are will only be apparent in the future.

Of more practical use, certainly for any Catholic struggling to establish exactly what the Catholic Church's position was on a range of issues connected with clerical sexual abuse, is a document issued in mid-May 2010 by the United States Conference of Catholic Bishops (USCCB). It gives a series of questions and answers that are readily available. Among the questions addressed are 'What happens after the bishop reports the results of the preliminary inquiry to the CDF?' 'What does a sexual abuse trial look like when conducted under Canon Law?' 'Does the CDF ever ask the Pope to impose a penalty?' It would be good to have copies of this in the library of every newspaper, radio and TV station. Factual information might help to reduce much of the ill-informed coverage. One current example of misinformation that created headlines around the world occurred in late June 2010.

The Vatican is currently doing its level best, through its lawyers, to remain at arm's length from the child-abuse scandal – at a legal arm's length, that is. An Oregon court had permitted the Holy See to be listed as a defendant in a clerical sexual abuse lawsuit. The Vatican's lawyers then appealed to the US Supreme Court, asking the court to summarily dismiss the action on a number of grounds but particularly on the argument that the Foreign Sovereign Immunity Act protects the Holy See from liability unless the abused victim can demonstrate that the priest who abused him was acting as an employee of the Vatican.

The Supreme Court declined to make a ruling one way or the other. The legal action now reverts back to the Oregon court for legal arguments to be heard at that level. Thus the Oregon court will now hear arguments that the Pope and the Vatican can be included as defendants. While the news media whipped up a great deal of froth on a non-story, life at a lower level continues. Forty-seven-year-old Peter Caffrey, formally of Springfield, Massachusetts, has filed suit against two retired bishops, Joseph Maguire and Thomas Dupre, alleging that they failed to provide adequate supervision to a notorious abuser, Richard Lavigne. The abuse allegedly occurred at two locations: St Francis of Assisi Church and Lavigne's lakeside house. Lavigne was convicted of two counts of child abuse in 1992. Bishop Dupre was himself indicted for abusing two boys.

As Lavigne was defrocked from the priesthood in 2004 he now lacks the protective cloak of secrecy that is still such a feature of the sexual abuse scandal. For example, the current Archbishop of New York, Timothy Dolan, applied a curious criterion during his years at Milwaukee: the names of diocesan priests who were accused of sexual abuse on credible evidence were publicly posted; the names of Jesuits and other religious order priests were not made public.

There are currently moves from within the Catholic hierarchy to confront this issue. Teresa Kettlekamp, who has served as the executive director of the USCCB Office of Child and Youth Protection since 2005, has called on the Diocese of Kansas to release the names of clergy accused of sexually abusing children. Suppressing the names 'is not what we expected'.

Another who has joined the list of bishops who protected child-abusing priests is Bishop Tod Brown, who in 1990 wrote a letter recommending Father Ruben Garcia for a position in the Archdiocese of Tijuana. The bishop wrote the letter – which has only recently surfaced – despite being fully conversant with the priest's history, which included molesting boys in Idaho. Subsequently he was considered a problem priest in Boise to such an extent that he was sent as a repeat offender to the rehabilitation centre, the Servants of Paraclete. The continuing protection of Father Garcia gave him the freedom to continue abusing.

Clerical sexual abuse has become a modern Hydra: cut off one head and two new ones appear. Set up commissions of inquiry in one country and begin to address that country's problems, and the evil bursts out in not just one other location but many.

In February 2010, during a two-day meeting with the Irish hierarchy, Pope Benedict XVI denounced the sexual abuse of children by priests, and the failure of the Irish bishops to curb that abuse. The Pope and the Irish bishops and the top level of the Roman Curia concluded their meeting by openly acknowledging 'the failure of Irish Church authorities for many years to act effectively in dealing with cases involving the sexual abuse of young people by some Irish clergy and religious'. That failure on the part of the Irish hierarchy, the statement added, has caused 'a breakdown in trust in the Church's leadership and has damaged her witness to the Gospel and its moral teaching'. For Ireland one could substitute the names of a great many countries, as the following pages will confirm.

Quite a number of the abuse victims and their support organisations took great exception to the Pope's remarks describing the scandal as a 'failure of faith'. Maeve Lewis of the group One in Four complained that the Vatican had 'accepted no responsibility for its role in facilitating the sexual abuse of children'. The Pope had summoned all the Irish bishops to Rome in recognition of a crisis shaking the Church in that country after the release of the Murphy Commission Report. Talking directly to the assembled bishops, he said that 'sexual abuse of children is not only a heinous crime but also a grave sin which offends God and wounds the dignity of the human person created in his image'. Speaking at the conclusion of the meeting Cardinal Sean Brady of Armagh said the primary focus of the Irish hierarchy would be on the welfare of sexual abuse victims.

He detailed the plans of the Irish bishops to care for victims and to adopt 'best practices' programmes to protect children from abuse in the future.

Many in Ireland and further afield wondered about the continuance of Cardinal Brady as the leader of the Irish Church. 'How', they asked, 'could "best practices" programmes be implemented by a man who had himself been a party to the cover up of sexual abuse?' Brady had sworn two teenage victims of Father Brendan Smyth to secrecy in 1975 after recording their statements in a Church inquiry. Father Smyth was then free to continue abusing for a further eighteen years. The cardinal has recently explained that he was not the designated person to go to the Irish police, but he has also admitted to feeling ashamed that he had not always upheld the values that he professes and believes in. Cardinal Brady's failure to blow the whistle on an abusing priest in 1975 was destined to come back to haunt him.

Pope John Paul II saw clerical sexual abuse of the young as 'an American problem'. His successor appears to see it largely as an Irish problem, in the light of his trenchant criticism of the Irish Church. There has yet to be from the Pope or those gathered around him in the Vatican any serious examination of their own conduct. They point fingers but fail to look inwards at the failures in their own responses to this scandal engulfing the Catholic Church. Targeting a single country – be it the United States or Ireland – ignores the blinding reality. This scandal is global. Its roots do not reside in specific malfunctioning bishops working in a particular country. When studied, the pattern reveals identical characteristics in country after country. Simultaneously it is also a Vatican problem. Some public self-examination by Pope Benedict and others within the Vatican would be invaluable. They might begin by studying the following.

In April 2010 Archbishop Buti Tlhagale, head of the Archdiocese of Johannesburg and one of Africa's most prominent prelates, spoke openly regarding clerical sexual abuse not only in South Africa but throughout the continent. He warned that 'the misbehaviour of priests in Africa has not been exposed to the same glare of the media as in other parts of the world.' The archbishop made the following comments during his Chrism Mass homily:

'In our times we have betrayed the very Gospel we preach. The Good News we claim to announce sounds so hollow, so devoid of any meaning when matched with our much publicised negative moral behaviour . . . The image of the Catholic Church is virtually in ruins because of the bad behaviour of its priests, wolves wearing sheep's skin, preying on unsuspecting victims, inflicting irreparable harm, and continuing to do so with impunity. We are slowly but surely bent on destroying the Church of God by undermining and tearing apart the faith of lay believers.

'. . . I wish I could say that there are only a few bad apples. But the outrage around us suggests that there are more than a few bad apples . . . As Church leaders, we become incapable of criticising the corrupt and immoral behaviour of the members of our respective communities. We become hesitant to criticise the greed and malpractices of civil authorities. We are paralysed and automatically become reluctant to guide young people in the many moral dilemmas they face.'

In Australia, Archbishop Mark Coleridge of Canberra took to the Radio National airwaves in May 2010. Discussing the issue of clerical sexual abuse, he observed,

'No one can deny the scale of the problem and the urgent task. In the past, Church leaders were deflected from discussion of the topic by a misguided sense that silence could protect the Church from scandal.'

On 17 June 2010, Father David O'Hearn of the Australian Diocese of Maitland-Newcastle was charged with seventeen counts of abuse committed against five boys. Within the evidence submitted on behalf of Father O'Hearn, Vincent Ryan – the pastor of the parish where O'Hearn had served – claimed that he 'didn't hear anything about Father O'Hearn or another assistant priest in relation to children'. Vincent Ryan is currently serving a prison sentence for abusing dozens of boys over a twenty-year period, prompting a multi-million-dollar compensation payment to his victims. In the statement that he made from his prison cell on behalf of Father O'Hearn he helpfully added, 'They would have been unaware of my behaviour either.' Court documents established that there had been concerns over the behaviour of Father O'Hearn between 1995 and 1997. The offences he has now been charged with date back to the 1980s. He is due to stand trial in the near future.

On 2 July 2009, in the Sydney District Court, Father John Denham was found guilty of a total of 134 sexual offences relating to thirty-nine boys. The 134 charges included buggery and multiple counts of indecent assault. These were not Denham's only victims, merely those who signed a statement for the police. They and the untold other victims should have been protected against abuse from Denham. His previous sole conviction for sexual abuse occurred much earlier in his career and only came to light when the victim contacted the police in 1997. At the subsequent trial Denham was found guilty of indecent assault and given a two-year jail sentence which was suspended.

Just as the many previous complaints to the Catholic

authorities had been ignored by the Church so now they
brushed the conviction to one side and continued to use
Father Denham as relief priest in various parishes. This
priest's earlier life bears examination. Father Denham was
recruited as a noviciate in the 1960s and, according to court
testimony, his sexual abuse of children began at that time.
Complaints made about his behaviour in the 1970s to
Church authorities were ignored. At St Pius X College at
Adamstown, Denham became well known for his habit of
touching boys indecently. Nearly all the victims were from
devout Catholic families and some were, in Judge Syme's
words, 'particularly targeted as especially vulnerable children' because of family circumstances and personal fragility. After a complaint by the mother of one of the pupils in
1979 Denham was transferred to work in the Charlestown
parish, then in 1981 transferred again to Taree, a coastal
town north of Newcastle. During his years in these parishes
he regularly committed sexual attacks on boys.

His behaviour, once he had been transferred to the St Pius
X Catholic High School in Newcastle in 1975, was incessant. He became head of discipline at the school, an
appointment comparable to giving a compulsive eater access to a chocolate factory. His pursuits included calling a
victim's name over the school intercom system with the
demand that the named individual 'come to Father Denham's private quarters'. He repeatedly anally raped boys
either in his office or in his quarters, then sent them back
into the classroom. He performed oral sex on countless
victims, caned others until they cried and then sexually
abused them. He talked to two seven-year-old victims about
Jesus, squeezing their genitals as they sat on his lap in the
school office. Syme advised the jury, 'The offender gave
both boys a chocolate before they left.'

Occasionally, Denham would ply young boys with
alcohol before assaulting them. He sexually abused one

drunken lad as the youth drove a car. He assaulted others on trips to a country presbytery as another priest watched. He bit one 'particularly vulnerable child' on the buttocks in the school corridor. Meanwhile, he enjoyed total protection from the principal of the school, Father Thomas Brennan. The trial judge observed, 'He [Father Brennan] at best took no action, and at worst caned the boys who complained. On one occasion this occurred even after a complaint from the parents.'

In 2009, when the appalling truth was established, Brennan was convicted of making a false written statement to protect Denham and placed on a twelve-month good behaviour bond. This case is a landmark in Australia. Because the Church authorities had been warned during Denham's career that he was committing sexual offences against children, and his superiors disregarded those warnings and retained Denham within the priesthood, thus allowing him to continue to harm and damage the young, the victims will now be able to mount civil actions against the Catholic Church in Australia.

Father Denham was sentenced to a maximum term of nineteen years and ten months, with a non-parole period of thirteen years and ten months. Born in 1942, he will remain in prison until his eightieth year.

In Austria the rank-and-file Catholics continue to resign and walk away from their Church. As previously recorded, this widespread desertion had initially been triggered by Pope John Paul II's refusal to remove Cardinal Groer from his post. The late Pope angrily dismissed the overwhelming evidence that established that Groer was a highly active paedophile. For every year that Karol Wojtyla ignored the evidence, tens of thousands left the Church. Eventually, when he bowed to reality, it was too late: the desertions continue up to the present day. In the past two years 90,000 people have removed their names from Catholic Church registries; the Austrian bishops anticipate a similar loss in the current year. Overwhelmingly the reason has remained constant: the disgust at clerical sexual abuse and the failure of the Vatican in general and Pope Benedict in particular to take more effective action than uttering hand-wringing apologies.

Vienna's Cardinal Christoph Schonborn has introduced new policies designed to curb sexual abuse by Austrian priests. 'The wall of silence must be broken. The abuse scandal cannot be allowed to repeat itself.' Reflecting early in 2010, Schonborn recalled discussing the problem of his predecessor Cardinal Groer with Cardinal Ratzinger and that the then head of the CDF had told him that he wanted to set up a fact-finding commission with regard to the many allegations swirling around Groer 'to establish clarity'. 'To me,' Schonborn reported, 'that is one of the best indications that today's Pope had a very decisive, clear way of handling abuse cases'.

Subsequently, Ratzinger had indicated that his commission was a non-starter. In the heart of the Vatican circa 1995 there was not a demand for clarity on this particular issue: 'The other side, the diplomatic side, had prevailed.' Surely this is a veiled reference to the then Secretary of State, Cardinal Sodano. When it came to matters of the mind and intellectual concepts, such as Liberation Theology, Ratzinger went for the target until he had destroyed it. Matters of the flesh were something different. Homosexuality? Attack. Clerical sexual abuse? Dither.

Belgium has a particular dark history regarding child abuse. This is the country of Marc Dutroux, who was arrested in 1996 and charged with kidnapping, torturing and sexually abusing six young girls, four of whom died. He is currently serving a life sentence. From that nightmare the Belgian nation developed a greater sensitivity to the issue of sexual abuse of children. An independent Commission was established in 2000 to deal with all allegations of sexual abuse by priests. The large brick wall erected by the Catholic Church's hierarchy in Belgium very successfully thwarted much of the Commission's work. A mere thirty-three cases were dealt with in ten years, a tribute to the obduracy of Catholic officialdom in Belgium.

Several factors have ensured that the Belgium paedophiles and their protectors are now finally feeling increasing heat. A new president of the Commission, President Professor Adriaenssens has a string of impressive qualifications and great experience of the problem; he also has excellent connections. With sexual abuse cases gaining increasing prominence in nearby Germany and the Netherlands, twenty new cases were reported in Belgium during the first four months of 2010, but what really transformed the level of reported cases were two events that occurred on 23 April. The first was the announcement by the Bishop of Bruges, Roger Vangheluwe, that he was resigning because of the revelation that he had sexually abused a boy.

On the same day, an interview on television by Archbishop André-Joseph Léonard of Mechelen-Brussels, recently appointed the primate of Belgium, electrified the entire nation. Archbishop Léonard declared, 'From today the Belgian Church has turned over a new leaf from a not very distant past when such matters would pass in silence or be concealed.' During the course of the next month over 400 abuse allegations flooded in. Many believed that things were going to be different from that day. They may not have appreciated just how very different it was going to get.

If the Belgian hierarchy had been shaken by the first four months of 2010, the events of 24 June had the Catholic establishment spinning like a top. The headquarters of the Belgian Catholic Church was raided by a team of police officers. They entered the archbishopric at 10.30 a.m. when the monthly meeting of the Episcopal Conference was in progress. They informed the gathering that they were investigating complaints of sexual abuse which were alleged to have taken place 'within the territory of the archdiocese'. The palace of the archbishop was subsequently sealed. All documents and mobile phones were confiscated and the bishops were advised that nobody could leave the building. Everyone within was interrogated.

The police were extremely busy on this particular day. Apart from the archdiocese they also raided the home of retired Archbishop Godfried Danneels in Mechelen, seizing documents and a computer. The offices of the independent Commission were also raided and all files seized. The tombs of Cardinals Jozef-Ernest Van Roey and Leon Joseph Suenens were searched. The bishops and their staff were held until 7.30 p.m.

When news reached the Vatican, the Pope talked of the 'regrettable methods' used by the police. His Secretary of State was less diplomatic, describing the raids as 'serious and unbelievable', and moved into hyperbole, comparing the raids to the practices of the communist regimes. As the days went by, the steam from the archdiocese and the Vatican mounted, displaying a profound ignorance of the law. The only buildings in Belgium for which the Vatican could claim diplomatic immunity were the home and offices of the papal nuncio. The reaction displays that same concept of immunity that has dogged the issue of clerical sexual abuse of the young. The Church had long considered that its priests, bishops and cardinals did not have to report such abuse to the civil authorities. In this they demonstrated either blissful ignorance of the law or an arrogant indifference to it. The investigations continue.

Across the border in the Netherlands, there has also been a recent explosion of reported sexual abuse by clerics. In early March 2010 Radio Netherlands reported that 137 priests and religious faced charges of sexual abuse. Later the same month came a report of 600 allegations of clerical sexual abuse being recorded within a four-week period. The figures represent an extraordinary surge in a country with a historically low figure for reported abuse. Subsequently the Dutch Catholic Church specifically created a unit to deal with alleged clerical sexual abuse. 'Help and Justice' revealed that it had received 'more than 1,000 claims of sexual abuse' since the first allegations came to light in late February. Dates of the alleged abuses ranged from the 1960s through to more recent times.

The retired Archbishop of Utrecht, Cardinal Adrianus Simonis, declared himself 'extremely shocked' and 'ashamed'. He said that he had been aware of no more than ten cases in his four decades as a bishop. 'If a priest was involved, I was responsible', he said. 'If it was a member of a religious order, it was up to the order itself.'

The Bishop of Rotterdam, Ad Van Luyn, when questioned about the issues that these revelations raised, confirmed that he knew of concrete cases during his time as head of the Salesian Order between 1975 and 1981. This was the first time that the bishop had admitted knowing about such abuse during the period when he was in charge. He has now called for an independent inquiry. One of the first to be investigated will be the bishop himself.

In Chile, the Cardinal of Santiago elected to go the direct route with regard to investigating abuse allegations. Confronted with complaints from eight men accusing the Reverend Father Fernando Karadima Farina of abusing them in the confessional, the cardinal has asked the Congregation for the Doctrine of Faith to conduct the investigation. With the applications for such investigations creating an increasingly long tailback he may be waiting quite a while for a response.

There are certain features that recur with this scandal.

Some of these relate to the secret system of hiding the abusing priest among unaware and unsuspecting members of the faithful in a different environment. One of the other features is the resistance put up by the Catholic hierarchy to accept their responsibilities when their guilt has been established. The Irish abuses contain this element; among others that share this stubborn bloody-mindedness are at least some of the Canadian clergy.

Earlier in this book I have described how the Christian Brothers of Mount Cashel clearly regarded themselves as above the law for years. It appeared by 1988 that the various erring prelates in Newfoundland had accepted their fate and were resigned to making adequate compensation to the victims. One exception was the Roman Catholic Church in St John's. In 1989 the Reverend James Hickey was found guilty of sexually abusing eight altar boys while he was parish priest at the Burin Peninsula in the late 1970s. He was sentenced to five years' imprisonment. For ten years from 1999 to 2009 the eight boys, now grown men, and their lawyer Greg Stack battled for justice. Despite the criminal conviction of Hickey, the Church fought them every inch of the way, stubbornly arguing that the Church was not liable.

Finally, in February 2009 the former altar boys heard the Newfoundland Supreme Court rule that the Church was indeed liable for the sexual abuse of the eight boys by Hickey. The struggle for compensation then began. In mid-December 2009, twenty years after Father Hickey was convicted, the Church finally agreed to settle one of the lawsuits for $200,000. One down; seven to go.

After a number of years, during which the Pope's home country of Germany continually posted extremely low figures for clerical sexual abuse, in 2010 the dam broke, in the wake of a number of scandals. In February, the head of the German Bishops' Conference, Archbishop Robert

Zollitsch, publicly apologised to the victims who had been systematically abused by two priests at a Jesuit school in Berlin. It was estimated that 120 former students had allegedly been abused at some seven schools throughout the nation. Bishop Walter Mixa of Augsburg partly attributed the abuse to 'the sexual revolution'. That drew from the country's Justice Minister, Sabine Leutheusser-Schnarrenberger, the observation that the bishop was 'hiding behind polemic excuses instead of contributing to clearing up the crisis'.

With the scandal growing by the day, the Jesuits contracted a special investigator to establish the facts. The Catholic Church set up an abuse hotline. It opened for business on 2 April. It closed – at least temporarily – the same day, after crashing under the weight of the phone traffic: 4,459 callers before the system went into meltdown. The same month Bishop Mixa was exposed as an alcoholic who had made homosexual advances to two priests. There were various other allegations as the now former bishop was left to consider sexual revolutions.

By May 2010 the Jesuits' investigator, Ursula Raue, was able to report that she had so far established that at least 205 former students claimed to have been abused; she thought the final figure would be even higher: 'We cannot expect to have heard everything yet.' She further revealed that forty-six Jesuits and a number of lay staff had been accused of abuse or of knowing of such crimes and failing to act. By June there were calls for the creation of an independent Commission comparable to the Irish model. The German Government, meanwhile, were closely monitoring the situation. Chancellor Angela Merkel had remarked earlier in the year that 'child abuse is one of the most terrible crimes and has to be investigated. I have the impression the Catholic Church has realised this.' Quite what the German Pope was making of all these revelations in his

home country is difficult to gauge. More food for thought
came this time from Spain.

The Spanish psychologist Pepe Rodriguez has researched and written at great length on the subject of
clerical sexual abuse. His conclusions, published in several books, are compelling. Compared with other countries that have a large percentage of Roman Catholics,
Spain's official figures for clerical sexual abuse have
historically been very low. Either the Spanish Church
has operated the most efficient cover-up in the world or
there is another, as yet, unrevealed explanation. Dr
Rodriguez's careful research may well supply that explanation. His studies show that in traditionally Catholic
Spain, 60 per cent of priests are sexually active, in
violation of their vows of celibacy. Of these, his study
found that 53 per cent had relations with adult females,
21 per cent with adult males, 14 per cent with underage
males and 12 per cent with underage females. Dr
Rodriguez records the fact that a large number of Spanish
priests leave the priesthood to marry and that others
form long-term relationships that are ignored by both the
laity and the Church hierarchy.

The Vatican is currently investigating fourteen cases of
alleged child abuse in Spain committed by priests over the
past nine years: an average of less than two cases a year.
Monsignor Charles Scicluna, who is the Vatican's 'promoter of justice' – effectively the prosecutor for the CDF –
described Spain as 'one of the countries with the lowest
number of alleged abuse investigations.' Scicluna may have
been tempting fate. In mid-May 2010 it was revealed that
the head of the Francis of Assisi Centre in Cordoba and
three other staff members had been accused of sexual abuse;
there is also evidence of a Church cover-up. One thing is
certain: the traditionally very close relationship between
Church and State in Spain – a relationship reaching back

many decades – would have made it very difficult for abuse victims in Spain to denounce a priest.

At much the same time as the revelations in Cordoba were occurring in May, the most senior prelate in Italy, Cardinal Angelo Bagnasco, admitted the 'possibility' that clerical sexual abuse cases had been covered up on the Pope's doorstep. He suggested that Italian Church officials 'may have sometimes been inclined to protect the Church rather than reporting cases to the police'. His number two, Monsignor Mariano Crociata, went further: 'There have been about 100 clerical sex abuse cases over the past decade.' He declined to state how many priests had been prosecuted or defrocked. The same week, a priest in Savonna went on trial for alleged sexual violence against a twelve-year-old girl, and a seventy-three-year-old Milan priest, Father Domenico Pezzini, a leading supporter for gay rights, was arrested for allegedly abusing a thirteen-year-old boy. In September 2009 in Verona, seventy-three priests were accused of sexually abusing 235 minors. Previously sixty-seven students at an institute for the deaf had alleged that 'abuse, paedophilia and corporal punishment occurred at the school from the 1950s to the 1980s at the hands of the Congregation for the Company of Mary', and in June 2010 yet another high-profile Italian cleric, Father Pierino Gelmini, was accused of abusing twelve young men at a drug rehabilitation centre. These various incidents pose serious questions to a hierarchy that quotes a figure of ten cases per year.

It seems that wherever one turns, no matter which country one considers, there is significant evidence of clerical sexual abuse. One might not expect alarm bells to be ringing among the Swiss bishops, but they are. In June 2010, the country's bishops toughened their stance against clerical sexual abuse by announcing that offenders will be systematically reported to the police. Previously they reported only the most serious cases and merely encouraged victims to file complaints with the police and to get help from victim consultation centres. Between January and June 2010, 104 victims have come forward. Their cases involve seventy-two priests. In March the Swiss Bishop's Conference admitted that it had 'underestimated' the scale of sexual abuse involving priests.

Through this global maelstrom, what of the Vatican? What of Pope Benedict XVI? How stands the epicentre of Christianity?

For quite a number of its residents within the Vatican City State, the Papacy of Benedict XVI had to all intents and purposes concluded by late 2009. They expect nothing of any lasting importance, no new policies or initiatives – at least not until after the next conclave elects Benedict's successor. Meanwhile, they attend quietly to their duties. Others were caught up in the tsunami that the global scandal of clerical sexual abuse had become. It is an infrastructure that is quintessentially medieval attempting to respond to a scandal that was not born in the late twentieth century but one whose roots went back many centuries. The Internet age has ensured that more information and greater truth has come to hand on this issue in the past twenty-five years than in the previous five hundred. Yet those tasked within the Vatican and beyond with responding to the demands not only for truth, but also for justice and total transparency were very largely at a loss as to how to respond.

The weight was on the shoulders of Father Federico Lombardi, the Director of the Vatican Press Office, assisted by a few colleagues. In the second half of 2009, it was finally acknowledged that a greater degree of professionalism was needed. The San Francisco-based company Meltwater, leading specialists in Internet media monitoring, were put under contract. It was the first step that the Press Office had ever taken into the twenty-first century. Meltwater seek then advise on the potential content for a Vatican response to damaging stories.

Above everything else, insiders realised that what was lacking was central direction. Before that could be achieved there would have to be a radically different incumbent on St Peter's throne. That change was beyond them for the present, other changes were not. Lombardi set about getting some heavyweights on board. These included Archbishop Claudio Maria Celli, President of the Pontifical Council for Social Communications, and Giovanni Maria Vian editor-in-chief for *L'Osservatore Romano*, the Vatican newspaper, which continues from time to time to print what the Pope ought to have said rather than what he actually did say. This team, who had previously ploughed separate furrows, first acknowledged that the world's news media were not particularly interested in an organisation that often took months to respond to an issue. Now the Vatican response is on a daily basis. Any visitor to the Vatican website will find that it has benefited from updates, for good measure there is now also a Twitter page. Spin has always been part of the Vatican armoury; now they have embraced techniques more usually found in the press departments of Downing Street and the White House. The object was for the Vatican to 'create its own narrative' of the clerical sexual abuse crisis.

The Pope's former congregation, the CDF, has been considering for more than two years amending Canon Law with a view to giving the Pope the power to cut through the drawn-out tortuous process that removing a bishop currently involves. The overriding problem is the lack of leadership from the top. As one long-serving bishop put it to this author in the closing days of 2009:

'Too many of us are unduly preoccupied lamenting low birth rates, materialism and relativism. The Holy Father was talking last week about the temptations of secularisation, hedonism, the fragility of families, etc, etc. They are all important issues but until we deal with clerical sex abuse and really deal with it, we are largely wasting our time discussing the other items on the shopping list.'

As the New Year progressed, the 'tsunami', far from diminishing, had developed a life force of its own. While the bishops in Germany, Austria and Holland and further afield struggled to come to terms with increasing numbers claiming that they had been abused, their respective governments looked to Catholicism's ultimate leadership. By early March 2010, German Justice Minister Sabine Leutheusser-Schnarrenberger had grown tired of waiting. She expressed her frustration, talking of what she saw as 'the Vatican building a wall of silence on the issue of clerical sexual abuse'. Father Federico Lombardi was quickly out of the traps, defending the Church's response to sexual abuse complaints and rejecting the charge made by the minister. He talked of how Germany, Austria and Holland had responded with 'timely and decisive action' and of how their bishops had shown 'a desire for transparency' by inviting victims to come forward with their stories. He continued:

'By doing so they have approached the matter "on the right foot" because the correct starting point is recognition of what has happened and concern for the victims and the consequences of the acts committed against them.'

Lombardi then weakened his argument by citing child

abuse outside the Catholic faith: 'In Austria, for example, there have been 510 recent reports of abuse, only seventeen involved Church-related institutions.' In this first shot from the Vatican, though, Lombardi neglected to mention that in the same week two dioceses in Austria suspended five priests pending further investigation of allegations that they had molested students, and the Netherlands announced that it was opening a major investigation after more than 200 people came forward in two weeks, alleging they had been abused by priests.

The Vatican cause had hardly been helped less than two weeks previously when a sex scandal reaching into Pope Benedict's household was exposed. Angelo Balducci, a Gentleman of his Holiness, was caught on a wiretap ordering a male prostitute from Vatican chorister Thomas Ehiem. The transcripts of the tapes indicated that Ehiem had previously procured for Balducci at least ten contacts with, among others, 'two black Cuban lads', a former model from Naples and a rugby player from Rome. The Vatican Press Office declined to comment on the affair.

Putting that embarrassment to one side, it was readily apparent how much easier it had suddenly become for the news media to get access to a wide variety of Vatican figures. Monsignor Charles Scicluna, for example, is the 'promoter of justice' for the Congregation for the Doctrine of the Faith, effectively the prosecutor for the former Holy Office, Roman Catholicism's thought police. Scicluna does not normally give interviews, and those that he does give are hardly brimming with facts. Talking to the Catholic news agency Zenit on 14 March 2010, however, he was positively loquacious:

'. . . Between 1975 and 1985, I do not believe that any cases of paedophilia committed by priests were

brought to the attention of our Congregation. More-
over, following the promulgation of the 1983 Code of
Canon law, there was a period of uncertainty as to
which of the delicta graviora ['most serious crime'],
were reserved to the competency of this dicastery.
Only with the 2001 'motu proprio' did the crime of
paedophilia again become our exclusive remit.'

Which begs the question, who then between 1975 and
2001, within the Vatican was responsible for the investigation and subsequent action in cases involving clerical sexual
abuse of children?

Subsequently, Scicluna revealed a variety of statistics
covering the years 2001 to 2010: '. . . we have considered
accusations concerning around three thousand cases of
diocesan and religious priests, which refer to cases committed over the past fifty years.' The 3,000 cases covered
a variety of categories: '60 percent of the cases chiefly
involved sexual attraction towards adolescents of the
same sex, another thirty percent involved heterosexual
relations . . . the cases of priests accused of paedophilia in
the true sense have been about three hundred in nine
years.'

Monsignor Scicluna also made himself available to the
Italian bishops' newspaper *L'Avvenire*, where similar
ground was covered. The figures that the prosecutor
was quoting only refer, of course, to the cases that came
to the CDF; they represent a very small part of the
situation. The majority of cases never reached Rome
during the years referred to. As the evidence within this
book has demonstrated, a great many were simply covered
up and the offending priest moved to another location.
Archbishop Salvatore Fisichella, the President of the
Pontifical Academy for Life was another heavyweight
who found himself talking to the media at this time.

One particular remark of his was particularly important. 'The Pope wants to implement a "zero tolerance" policy regarding sexual abuse of minors, similar to the US Bishops' conference in 2002. That policy', the archbishop said, 'is a moral obligation.'

A global application of the policy, particularly if applied retrospectively to those who had covered up for an abusing priest, would throw up a great many vacancies – including the position of the head of the CDF. While serving in the United States the current holder of that post, Cardinal William Levada, had permitted at least four priests whom he knew had sexually abused children to remain in public ministry. As March progressed, articles and statements favourably disposed towards Pope Benedict were flowering everywhere, a tribute to the efforts of Father Lombardi and Celli and Maria Vian. The very long article in the *National Catholic Reporter* by John Allen, a long-time admirer of the Pope, came from a writer held in high regard within the Vatican, indeed so high was the regard for Allen's work that the entire piece was posted on Vatican Radio. The next contributor to this paean would have raised eyebrows on both sides of the Tiber:

'. . . The way that he responds [to confronting difficult situations] is remarkably efficient, at least for all those who are not guided by totally hostile sentiments, and it is efficient both for its humility and sincerity and for the sound reasoning of the Pope.

'The pastoral letter to the Irish is only the most recent example of his great charisma.'

The author of this and more in a similar vein was Prime Minister Silvio Berlusconi. Many receiving such praise from such a quarter might feel that their situation was more desperate than they had realised.

Another vote of approval came from Vatican analyst Marco Politi, writing in the left-wing newspaper *Il Fatto Quotidiano*:

> 'Over the course of the last fifteen years, there has been a sort of Copernican revolution within the Church. For centuries, the Church hid the facts because its main goal was to defend the Institution's prestige. Today, the Pope himself encourages speaking out.'

These are merely a sample of a very well-orchestrated campaign. Inevitably, the other side of the coin was also on display. Some of the news media were highly critical that within the pastoral letter that Benedict had written to the Catholics of Ireland there was no acknowledgement of any Vatican responsibility in the scandal and no specific punishments to be applied to erring bishops who were blamed, not only by the victims but also by the government-ordered investigations, for having covered up years of abuse and by doing so exacerbated the abuse.

Though Benedict had apologised profusely within his letter, the apology was third party. He shared 'the dismay and sense of betrayal that so many of you have experienced on learning of these criminal acts'. He had been head of the CDF from the early 1980s and then Pope – a period of more than a quarter of a century – yet, to judge from his eight-page letter, at no time did his actions, or lack of them, contribute one jot to the greatest disaster to befall the Church for more than five hundred years.

He rebuked the Irish bishops for 'grave errors of judgement' but did not criticise anyone within the Vatican, living or dead, not even his predecessor John Paul II, who protected several paedophiles, and had also encouraged secrecy and cover-up over such issues from his time as a Bishop of Cracow. Significantly, Wojtyla's great concern for the good name of 'Mother Church' – a concern that justified secrecy and cover – is a characteristic that Benedict shares.

In 1985 in Oakland, California, Bishop John S. Cummins was attempting to have a serial sex abuser, Father Stephen Kiesle, defrocked. He engaged in correspondence with the head of the CDF, Cardinal Ratzinger, an action which in itself would appear to contradict flatly the statements recorded earlier from Monsignor Scicluna that cases of paedophilia were not part of the CDF remit between 1975 and 2001. Responding to Bishop Cummins' letter of 13 September 1985, part of Ratzinger's response reads:

> 'This court, although it regards the arguments presented in favour of removal in this case to be of grave significance, nevertheless deems it necessary to consider the good of the Universal Church together with that of the petitioner and it is also unable to make light of the detriment that granting the dispensation can provoke with the community of Christ's faithful, particularly regarding the young age of the petitioner.
>
> 'It is necessary for this Congregation to submit incidents of this sort to very careful consideration which necessitates a longer period of time.'

Father Kiesle had been sentenced to three years' probation in 1978, after pleading 'no contest' to charges of lewd conduct for tying up and molesting two young boys in a San Francisco rectory. In 1981, he asked to leave the priesthood, a request supported by his diocese, which forwarded the papers to Rome. In 1982, Bishop Cummins had urged Ratzinger to grant the request. In 1985, it was still pending – hence the exchange of letters referred to above. It was 1987 before Father Kiesle was defrocked, he had meanwhile carried out volunteer work with children. He was arrested in 2002 and charged with thirteen counts of child molestation; all but two counts were dismissed on the grounds that they exceeded the statute of limitation. He was later sentenced to six years' imprisonment in 2004 for molesting a young girl in 1995.

In 1985, the current Pope's sole concerns with regard to this case were demonstrably that Kiesle should be provided 'with as much paternal care as possible' and that the Universal Church's good name should be protected.

The desire that such cases should be examined in great secrecy was enshrined by Ratzinger in a letter he wrote to every bishop in 2001, advising that all clerical sexual abuses were now officially within their remit and should be forwarded to the CDF and that this should be done with the greatest attention to complete secrecy.

When details of the Kiesle case became public in the first quarter of 2010, it became the latest scandal to draw a vast quantity of negative media coverage of the Vatican in general and Benedict in particular. The response team both inside and outside the Vatican was at pains in all of these various cases to disassociate the Pope from any responsibility. During 2010 he has become increasingly like T.S. Eliot's Macavity, with an ever ready alibi, he is always a long way from the scene of the crime protesting his innocence.

The Pope's pastoral letter to Ireland, like his entire papacy, had promised much but delivered very little. Saying sorry, acknowledging the hurt, accepting the Church's mistakes was well and good but the mistakes were not identified and any potential remedies not revealed. Rebuking the Irish bishops was justified; ignoring the fact that bishops in a great many other countries stood indicted was not.

If charity still begins at home so to should honesty. Some public criticism of one or two of his cardinals would not have gone amiss.

Cardinal Dario Castrillón Hoyos publicly boasted in 2010 about a letter he had written to a French bishop, congratulating him for not reporting a paedophile priest to the authorities. The priest in question, Father René Bissey, was convicted in October 2000 for sexual abuse of eleven minor boys between 1989 and 1996. Castrillón wrote to Bishop Pierre Pican:

> 'I rejoice to have a colleague in the Episcopate that, in the eyes of history and all the other bishops of the world, preferred prison than denounce one of his sons and priest.'

On 16 April 2010 Castrillón spoke at a conference on the 'legacy of John Paul II' at a Catholic university in Murcia, Spain. He told the audience that he had shown the letter to the late Pope prior to posting it. John Paul II had applauded the act and authorised Castrillón to send it.

Benedict's apparent reluctance to take men like Cardinal Castrillón to task might be because, according to Castrillón, the letter 'was the outcome of a high-level meeting of cardinals', as he told RCN Radio. 'Therefore, the current Pope, who at the time was a cardinal, was present.' That would lend credence to a view held by many within the Vatican that the position of Pope Benedict on the issue of clerical sexual abuse has undergone a sea change. It is not only sections of the news media who believe that Benedict has come very late to his current position on clerical sexual abuse.

Cardinal Sodano, the previous Secretary of State, and Cardinal Bertone, the current holder of that office, are just two who are vulnerable on the issue of clerical sexual abuse.

Both men were great champions of the founder of the Legionaries of Christ, Marcial Maciel. Both men are alleged to have received large cash gifts from Maciel. On the evidence of the then Cardinal Ratzinger and Cardinal Schönborn, Sodano had persuaded Pope John Paul II to intervene and halt a Vatican investigation.

In mid-April 2010 in Chile, the old school – in the shape of Cardinal Bertone – weighed in with his views on clerical sexual abuse. He dismissed the view that priestly celibacy was one of the causes of child sexual abuse but he knew what was. 'Many psychologists and psychiatrists have demonstrated that there is no relation between celibacy and paedophilia. They do however believe that there is a relationship between homosexuality and paedophilia.' As Jim Fitzgerald, executive director of Call to Action, a Catholic movement working for equality and justice in the Church and society observed: 'Even the Pope, during his 2008 visit to the United States, said this crisis is not about gays and lesbians.'

On Palm Sunday 2010, the Pope gave clear indication that the pressure of the sexual abuse crisis was getting to him. During the course of his sermon he said, 'Faith in God helps lead one towards the courage of not allowing oneself to be intimidated by the petty gossip dominant opinion.' This was interpreted by the majority of his listeners as a clear reference to the sexual abuse scandal. By Easter, Sodano and Bertone were rapidly becoming a mordant double act. This time it was Sodano's turn. During the Easter Sunday Mass, lifting a phrase from the Pope's Palm Sunday remarks, he described the global controversy as amounting to no more than 'petty gossip'. Two days before, on Good Friday, the Pope's personal preacher had likened the criticism being levelled at the Catholic Church over child abuse to the 'collective violence suffered by the Jews'.

Notwithstanding every effort of the Vatican spin doctors and friendly news media, the opinion polls indicated their endeavours had failed. A CBS poll measuring papal 'unfavourability', showed a staggering rise in ratings against the Pope in the last four years, from 4 to 24 per cent. In the Pope's home country a *Stern* magazine poll showed that confidence in Benedict had collapsed from 62 per cent at the end of January to 39 per cent at the end of March. A few weeks after those polls, Benedict observed, 'This sex scandal is a test for me and the Church.' With accusations continuing in the media, alleging that the Pope had helped cover up the actions of paedophile priests to save the Church's reputation, the Vatican public relations trio were made well aware that their counter-attack was faltering. At least one section of it was proving counterproductive.

Vatican Radio quoted Cardinal Giovanni Lajolo, a Holy See official, as saying that the Church must pardon its attackers for what he called 'hatred against the Catholic Church'. Spanish Cardinal Julián Herranz, who heads a Vatican disciplinary commission, asserted that 'the Pope is being attacked because of his stands against abortion and same-sex marriage. Powerful lobbies want to impose a different agenda.' Cardinal José Saraiva Martins, aide to the Pope weighed in with: 'This is a pretext for attacking the Church . . . There is a well organised plan with a very clear aim.'

What was very obvious was that a fortress mentality now existed within the higher levels of the Church. The Vatican trio had not been idle. During the last days of April 2010, a three-day communications conference was held. Apart from a large quantity of priests and Church officials from a number of countries who were seeking fresh ideas of how to respond to their various constituencies, there were guest speakers. A public relations consultant talked and demonstrated how Italian companies managed crises when confronted with a welter of bad publicity. A US branding expert talked about the challenge of managing 'one of the oldest and most complex brands out there' – his definition of Christianity. On the final day of the conference, when over 100 people squeezed into the Vatican press room, they had one dominant question to put to Father Lombardi: 'How should we respond to the kind of coverage the Church is getting?' Lombardi acknowledged that 'the past two months has been particularly intense.' The answer, he said, was not to prevaricate, or dissemble. 'What is called for is maximum transparency.' He added, 'You must reduce the perception that we have a secretive culture, or something to hide.' Coming after many years marked by a secretive culture and cover-up, such advice poses a fundamental question regarding the ability or otherwise of a leopard changing its spots.

Several weeks later, the Pope set an excellent example for his spin doctors to follow. In mid-May 2010, while being flown to Portugal he responded to reporters' questions, Father Lombardi having taken the precaution of having the questions submitted in advance of the flight. The Church's original stance that there was a media campaign against the Catholic Church plus an attack from the pro-choice and pro-gay marriage lobbies had been abandoned. Instead, the Pope now pointed the finger inwards at his own Church and the abusers. 'What is needed is a profound purification to end the greatest persecution the Church has endured.' He continued, 'the Catholic Church had always suffered problems of its own making, today we see it in a truly terrifying way.'

There had been other signs that finally the Vatican was listening before reacting. A summary of the new rules and procedures to be followed when dealing with a child abuser was published; it included changes that many had been asking for over the years. It is now mandatory for such cases to be reported to the police. In the most serious cases Pope Benedict will defrock priests without going through the process of a Church trial. There were several other new guidelines, all designed to ensure that the process would be streamlined and strengthened.

At the end of May 2010 the Vatican gave details of the Apostolic Visitation to Ireland that had been promised earlier in the year. Commencing in the autumn, four senior prelates would each descend on an Irish archdiocese to individually and collectively 'explore more deeply, questions concerning the handling of cases of abuse, taking as their terms of reference various guidance documents that contain the range of rules, laws and regulations that apply to prevention and possible improvements to current procedures regarding clerical sexual abuse'. After an exhaustive investigation, analysis and recommendations, they will move on to the next four dioceses. It is an initiative that deserves to be welcomed and one that should be replicated throughout the world wherever there has been a significant problem. It should also be applied nearer to home, within the Vatican, to ensure that some of the dead wood is removed.

There are many problems that beset the Church, some were listed by the Pope during a meeting with a group of Belgium bishops earlier in 2010:

'The diminution in the number of baptised people who openly bear witness to their faith and their membership of the Church, the gradual increase in the average age of priests and religious, the lack of ordained and consecrated people who work in the fields of pastoral, educational and social care, the scant numbers of candidates to the priesthood and consecrated life.'

Whether all or any of these can be reversed in the short term is unlikely. Perhaps when the many hundreds of thousands who have left the Church as a direct result of the scandal of clerical sexual abuse can see that the various reforms have been implemented with vigour the tide may turn.

Earlier in this book the details of the primate of Ireland Cardinal Sean Brady's unacceptable role in the cover-up of Father Brendan Smyth's crimes are recorded. Marie McCormack, one of this priest's victims, has accepted an out-of-court settlement reported to be in excess of $300,000. She has also accepted apologies from the various defendants, including Cardinal Brady, who at this time of writing continues to cling to high office. The current global cost of clerical sexual abuse since Father Gilbert Gauthe was first arrested in Louisiana in June 1983 currently stands at over $8 billion.

No sooner does one begin to feel the first stirrings of optimism with regard to the Church's future than the Vatican shoots itself in the foot, if not the head. On 15 July 2010, the Holy Office published a revised edition of the 2001 norms dealing with clerical abuse of minors and other 'exceptionally serious crimes against faith and mor- ality'. The revisions in Canon Law as they apply to child abuse are to be applauded, including as they do making an offence of looking at child pornography. Lumped into the same decree, however, is 'the attempted ordination of women'. This is now defined by Rome as 'one of the gravest crimes in Church law on a par with clerical child abuse'.

As of now, many people across the world would not allow an unaccompanied child to enter a Roman Catholic Church. The Catholic Church in England and Wales and in other countries feels obliged to ban priests from being alone with a child. The late Pope John Paul II and his advisors instructed priests throughout the world to avoid getting into 'risky situations with the opposite sex' and to 'use caution' when dealing with women parishioners because of 'sexual temptations'. Many of the sexually abusive priests are treated with injections of Depo-Provera, a drug frequently prescribed as a female contraceptive.

Recently a Rome-based prelate observed to me, 'There will not be, either in the short or medium term, a policy of zero tolerance with regard to the sex abusers. If such a policy existed and was applied across the board, irrespective of position, there are many bishops who would be forced to resign . . . many cardinals who would have to take early retirement . . . As for zero tolerance towards homosexuals, we already have that. It just happens to be confined to the laity. If it were applied to the priesthood, the infrastructure would collapse.'

All of these things have come to pass within 'the one true Church' under the leadership of the late Pope John Paul II, closely assisted by Joseph Ratzinger who has now become the last absolute monarch on earth.

Speaking in a series of meditations on Good Friday 2005, the then Cardinal Ratzinger said, 'How much filth there is in the Church, and even among those who, in the priesthood, ought to belong entirely to Christ!'. On 11 August 2010, however, Pope Benedict XVI let it be announced that he had not accepted the resignations of two of the bishops from the Archdiocese of Dublin, namely Bishops Walsh and Field. They, along with every single auxiliary bishop within the Dublin diocese, had been found guilty by the Murphy Commission of having knowledge of incidents of clerical sexual abuse and yet keeping their eyes and their mouths shut. The filth that so concerned Ratzinger five years ago is now considered by the Pope to be acceptable.

'At the same time came the disciples unto Jesus, saying, Who is the greatest in the kingdom of heaven?

2 And Jesus called a little child unto him, and set him in the midst of them,

3 And said, Verily I say unto you, Except ye be converted, and become as little children, ye shall not enter into the kingdom of heaven.

4 Whosoever therefore shall humble himself as this little child, the same is greatest in the kingdom of heaven.

5 And whoso shall receive one such little child in my name receiveth me.

6 But whoso shall offend one of these little ones which believe in me, it were better for him that a millstone were hanged about his neck, and that he were drowned in the depth of the sea.'

St Matthew 18: 1–6

Acknowledgements

To the many victims who talked to me; to the priests in a number of countries who confided in me; and to the many men and women who gave me such valuable assistance: I would like to thank all of you.

Bibliography

BOOKS:

'*Be Not Afraid!*' *André Frossard In Conversation With John Paul II*, André Frossard, The Bodley Head, London And St Martin's Press 1984

A Catholic Dictionary Containing Some Account Of The Doctrine, Discipline, Rites, Ceremonies, Councils, And Religious Orders Of The Catholic Church, William E. Addis and Thomas Arnold, Virtue & Co. Ltd, London 1928

A Catholic Myth: The Behaviour And Beliefs Of American Catholics, Andrew M. Greeley, Collier Books, Macmillan, New York 1990

A Democratic Catholic Church: The Reconstruction Of Roman Catholicism, Eugene C. Bianchi and Rosemary Radford, Crossroad, New York 1992

A Documentary History Of Religion In America Since 1865, Second Edition, Edited By Edwin S. Gaustad, William B. Eerdmans Publishing Company, Grand Rapids 1993

A Secret World: Sexuality And The Search For Celibacy, A. W. Richard Sipe, Brunner-Mazel, New York 1990

Ad Limina Addresses: The Addresses Of His Holiness Pope John Paul II To The Bishops Of The United States

During Their Ad Limina Visits, March 5–December 9, 1988, Pope John Paul II, United States Catholic Conference, Washington DC, 1989

Amchurch Comes Out, The US Bishops, Pedophile Scandals And The Homosexual Agenda, Paul Likoudis, Roman Catholic Faithful Inc., Petersburg, Illinois 2002

Annuario Pontifico, per l'anno 2001, Città Del Vatican, Libreria Editrice Vaticana, Rome 2001

Beyond The Threshold: A Life In Opus Dei, María del Carmen Tapia, Continuum Publishing Group 1999

Beyond Tolerance: Child Pornography On The Internet, Philip Jenkins, New York University Press 2001

Churchgoing & Christian Ethics, Robin Gill, The Press Syndicate of the University of Cambridge, Cambridge, UK 1999

From A Far Country: The Story Of Karol Wojtyla Of Poland, A. Kijowski and J. J. Szczepanski, with the collaboration of Krzysztof Zanussi, Eri/Neff, Santa Monica, CA 1981

Fruitful And Responsible Love, Karol Wojtyla, St Paul Publications, Slough 1978

Future Church, A Global Analysis Of The Christian Community To The Year 2010, Dr Peter W. Brierley, Monarch Books And Christian Research, London 1998

In God's Name, David Yallop, Jonathan Cape, London 1984

Love And Responsibility, Karol Wojtyla (translated By H. T. Willetts) Ignatius Press, San Francisco 1993

Pedophiles And Priests, Philip Jenkins, Oxford University Press 1996

The 1917 Pio-Benedictine Code Of Canon Law In English Translation With Extensive Scholarly Apparatus Dr Edward Peters, Ignatius Press, San Francisco, CA 2001

The Anatomy Of The Catholic Church, Gerard Noel, Hodder and Stoughton, London 1980

The Book of Gomorrah, Mediaeval Source-book, St Peter Damian, translated by Owen J. Blum, OFM, The Catholic University of America Press 1990

The Code Of Canon Law In English Translation, Collins Liturgical Publications, London 1983

The Encyclicals Of Pope John Paul II, Pope John Paul II, Our Sunday Visitor Publishing Division, Huntington, Indiana 1996

The Pope And The New Apocalypse, The Holy War Against Family Planning, Stephen D. Mumford, Center For Research on Population and Security, Research Triangle Park, NC, 1986

The Ratzinger Report: An Exclusive Interview On The State Of The Church, Joseph Ratzinger and Vittorio Messori, Ignatius Press, San Francisco 1985

The Theology Of Marriage And Celibacy, St Paul Editions, Boston 1986

Turning Point For Europe? Cardinal Joseph Ratzinger, Ignatius Press, San Francisco 1994

LETTERS OF POPE JOHN PAUL II:

On combating abortion and euthanasia, 1991
Letter to Women, 1995

APOSTOLIC EXHORTATIONS
OF POPE JOHN PAUL II:

Familiaris Consortio   1981
Reconciliatio et Paenitentia   1984

APOSTOLIC CONSTITUTIONS CONSULTED:

Sacrae Disciplinae Leges   1983

CHURCH DOCUMENTS CONSULTED:

Lumen Gentium	1964
Nostra Aetate	1965
Dignitatis Humanae	1965
Gaudium Et Spes	1965

SYNODAL AND CONGREGATIONAL
DOCUMENTS CONSULTED:

Instruction On Certain Aspects Of The 'Theology Of Liberation', Congregation For The Doctrine Of The Faith, 1984

Notes On The Correct Way To Present The Jews And Judaism In Preaching And Catechesis In The Roman Catholic Church, Commission For Religious Relation With The Jews, 1995

Instruction On Christian Freedom And Liberation, Congregation For The Doctrine Of The Faith, 1986

Domum Vitae, Congregation For The Doctrine Of The Faith, 1987

Vademecum For Confessors Concerning Some Aspects Of The Morality Of Conjugal Life, Pontifical Council For The Family, 1997

We Remember: A Reflection On The Shoah, Commission For Religious Relations With The Jews, 1998

'Dominus Iesus' On The Unicity And Salvific Universality Of Jesus Christ And The Church – Declaration, Cardinal Joseph Ratzinger, Catholic Truth Society, Publishers to the Holy See, London 2000

Declaration On Procured Abortion, Congregation For The Doctrine Of The Faith, 1974

DEPOSITIONS/TRANSCRIPTS/LEGAL DOCUMENTS:

Diocesan records from Lafayette, covering Glenn Gastel *et al*, individually and on behalf of their minor child *versus* the Archdiocese of New Orleans and others including Father Gilbert Gauthe

The Sipe Report: A. W. Richard Sipe, *Executive Summary*, 1986

Confidential Crisis Proposal, by The Rev Thomas Doyle, OP, Ray Mouton and Dr Michael Peterson, 1985

Doyle-Demarest Legal Memo, May 1996

PERIODICALS – ORIGINS:

National Catholic Documentary Service, Washington, 1978–1983

Catholic World News Agency, 2000–2005

REPORTS:

Annual reports 2001 to 2009 compiled by the USCCB Secretariat of Child and Youth Protection, to ascertain diocesan/eparchial compliance with the bishops *Charter for the Protection of Children and Young*

Careful Selection And Training Of Candidates For The States Of Perfection And Sacred Orders by the Sacred Congregation of the Religious, February 1961

Crimine Sollicitationis, issued by Pope John XXIII outlining the procedure to be followed in cases of sexually abusing priests using the pretext of confession, 1962

John Jay College Of Criminal Justice Report On Clerical Sexual Abuse In The United States, 2004

John Jay report covering 1950 to 2002. A study analyzing

allegations of sexual abuse in Catholic dioceses in the
United States

*Le Moyne College/Zogby International 'Contemporary
Catholic Trends' Poll Report*, 2002

National Catholic Safeguarding Commission. Annual reports 2007 to 2010 for England and Wales

Nolan Report, April 2001

Report on *'The Problem Of The Sexual Abuse Of African
Religious In Africa And Rome'*, Sister Marie MacDo-
nald, 1998

Report on *'The Sexual Abuse Of Religious And Non-
Religious Women By Priests'*, Sister Maura O'Donohue,
MD, February 1994 (The above two reports were made
available to the author by Vatican sources.)

*Roman Catholic Clericalism, Religious Duress And Clerical
Sexual Abuse*, The Rev Thomas Doyle, March 2001

*The Catholic Priest In The United States: Psychological
Investigations*, Eugene Kennedy, PhD and Victor Heckler, PhD, 1972

The Crisis In The Catholic Church In The United States, a
report prepared by the *National Review Board for the
Protection of Children and Young People*, February
2004

The Ferns Report, October 2005: Irish Government inquiry
into over 100 allegations of child sexual abuse between
1962 and 2002 made against 21 priests operating under
the aegis of the Diocese of Ferns

The Murphy Report. Irish Government investigation
headed by Judge Yvonne Murphy to report on the
handling by Church and State authorities into a representative sample of allegations and suspicions of child
sexual abuse by clerics in the Archiocese of Dublin over
the period 1975 to 2004

*The Role Of The Church In The Causation And Treatment
And Prevention Of The Crisis In The Priesthood*, a

report based on the records of 1,500 priests treated for mental problems, Dr Conrad W. Baars, November 1971

The Ryan Report. Irish Government investigation headed by Judge Sean Ryan. A ten-year investigation into the alleged abuse at orphanages and industrial schools run by Catholic religious orders across the State

Through The Lens Of The Organisational Culture Perspective: A Descriptive Study Of American Catholic Bishops' Understanding Of Clergy, Sexual Molestation And Abuse By Children And Adolescents, Dr Barbara Susan Balboni: PhD dissertation (Boston North Eastern University) 1998

NEWSPAPERS, PERIODICALS AND ON-LINE SERVICES CONSULTED:

Austrian: including *Der Standard, Die kleine Zeitung, Die Presse, Format, Kirche Intern, Kronenzeitung, Kurier, profil* (made available by Dr Wolfgang R. Lehner, Vienna)

English-language: including *America, Commonweal, The Tablet, The Washington Post,*

French: *including La Croix, L'Express, Le Monde, Le Monde Diplomatique, Libération*

German: including *Berliner Kurier, Berliner Morgenpost, Der Spiegel, Die Zeit, Frankfurter Allgemeine Zeitung, Hamburger Abendblatt, Hamburger Morgenpost, Stuttgarter Zeitung, Süddeutsche Zeitung*

Ireland: including *Irish Times, Independent, Sunday Business Post, RTE News*

Italian: including *L'Osservatore Romano, Corriere della Sera, Famiglia Cristiana, Il Giornalino, Il Giorno, Il Mattino, Il Messaggero, Il Mondo, L'Espresso, La Nazione, La Repubblica, 30 Giorni, Zenit Agency, Chiesa, Esspresso*

Mexico: *Patrick Madrid*

Spanish: including *Avui, El Informador (Mexico), El Mundo, La Vanguardia, Tiempo de Hoy*

Swiss: including *Blick, Facts, L'Echo, Le Temps, Neue Zürcher Zeitung, Sonntagszeitung, Wochenzeitung*

Catholic World News Agency, 2000–2005

United Kingdom: including *The Times, Belfast Telegraph, Observer, Guardian, Daily & Sunday Telegraph, Financial Times*

USA: *including Associated Press, Boston Globe, National Catholic Reporter, New York Times, Washington Post, Chicago Tribune, Rutland Herald, Vermont, Catholic World News, Catholic News Agency, America Magazine, Los Angeles Times, The Day.Com, Joe Wojtas, Hartford Courant, CBS News, New York Daily News*

Vatican City State: *Vatican Information Service, L'Osservatore Romano*